Bringing Home *the* Seitan

100 Protein-Packed, Plant-Based Recipes for Delicious "Wheat-Meat" Tacos, BBQ, Stir-Fry, Wings and More

Kris Holechek Peters

Ulysses Press

Published in the United States by:
Ulysses Press
P.O. Box 3440
Berkeley, CA 94703
www.ulyssespress.com

ISBN13: 978-1-61243-608-1
Library of Congress Control Number: 2016934486

Printed in the United States by United Graphics Inc.
10 9 8 7 6 5 4 3 2 1

Acquisitions editor: Casie Vogel
Project editor: Alice Riegert
Managing editor: Claire Chun
Editor: Lauren Harrison
Proofreader: Renee Rutledge
Front cover design: Rebecca Lown
Cover artwork: broccoli seitan stir-fry © Peter Kim/shutterstock.com; red cup of food © marco mayer/shutterstock.com; seitan, red peppers, and potatoes © kitty/shutterstock.com
Interior design: whatdesign @ whatweb.com
Layout: Jake Flaherty

Distributed by Publishers Group West

To Jesse. Thanks for being the best culinary adventure companion and vegetable butcher I could ever ask for.

Contents

Introduction

This is not your grandma's "wheat meat." We've come such a long way in the world of meat substitutes that they've largely become their own genre. Seitan is a high-protein, versatile, magical substance that can take on many different textures and flavors. Whether you want to replicate an old meaty recipe from your past, make a meal that will please omnivores and herbivores alike, or just want to try something new and novel—seitan is where it's at.

The recipes included in here run the gamut from basics that can act as a springboard for your own creations to new spins on old favorites. Whatever you're hankering for, this book is filled with hearty, mouthwatering fare that will incorporate new textures, exciting flavors, and more protein into your kitchen.

Seitan has been around for a long time, but gained popularity in the U.S. in the 1970s as vegetarianism grew more widespread and people looked to the cuisines of other cultures for inspiration. The history of "wheat meat" goes back over a millennium to China, where they mastered the art of alternative proteins (think mock duck)—making seitan as old as some of the world's largest religions. It's been around a while. Since the early days, faux meats have only increased in popularity, as more and more companies refine flavors and textures to make meat substitutes taste better and become more readily available. But you don't need to have a huge lab or commercial kitchen to make delicious "meaty" treats. You can partake in the history of seitan's evolution with the recipes in this tasty tome using simple ingredients and your own kitchen.

Oh My Gluten!

It seems countercultural to be literally writing the book on gluten, doesn't it? Using the G-word has become close to swearing in our modern culture. Why would someone write a book where it's the main ingredient?

Gluten has certainly gotten a lot of press in recent years, but it's not new. It's the protein found naturally in wheat and some other grains. It's what binds our bread and makes seitan so toothsome and well-textured—and high in protein.

Despite how often you hear about gluten intolerance and allergies, true gluten sensitivity is very rare. If you are someone who is affected, this is not the book for you. But, the overwhelming majority of people *can* tolerate gluten well. It's not that gluten is some evil opponent; it's a natural form of protein that exists in wheat. Too much of anything—sugar, fat, protein, salt—is too much of a good thing. As with anything in life, all things in moderation.

Seitan has been cooked and consumed for longer than any of us can imagine (over 1,500 years). Rest assured, cooking with it has withstood the test of time. If you have questions or concerns about gluten intolerance, please talk to a nutritional or medical professional.

Know Your Proteins

There are a lot of different kinds of vegetarian proteins out there, and it can be confusing. Here's a breakdown to help clarify what you're eating:

Tofu: Tofu is created by culturing soy milk, so the beans have been blended with water, liquefied, and then coagulated using one of several types of processes and enzymes. It comes in a variety of degrees of firmness and is sold as either silken tofu (which has a creamy texture, regardless of firmness) or standard tofu (which is typically water-packed and has a more curd-like texture than silken).

Water-packed tofu should be drained and pressed before using to express any excess liquid, allowing it to absorb flavor and to cook better. Silken tofu should not be pressed, as its structure is too soft to withstand any pressure.

Tempeh: Tempeh is also a soy product, but it uses the whole soybean, often including other grains or beans. The resulting product is fermented and usually sold as a slab. On its own tempeh can have a bitter edge to its taste, which can be reduced or eliminated by letting it simmer a little in a small amount of water or by using a marinade. Tempeh has a nice, hearty texture and holds its shape well in cooking.

TVP: TVP, or textured vegetable protein, is a product of soy, created by processing the beans. It's dried and needs to be reconstituted in liquid. It's often used to add texture and protein to dishes, and on its own has a texture similar to very lean ground beef or turkey.

Soy curls: Similar to TVP, but slightly less processed and in much larger chunks, soy curls must be reconstituted with liquid. They make a good substitute for chicken and cook up easily.

Commercially made fake meat: The secret sauce of these products (think veggie burgers, hot dogs, and the like) varies, but they are often soy based, using either TVP or tofu, with some added wheat gluten for texture.

Seitan: In its most basic variation, seitan is wheat gluten with some seasoning and a little flour. Wheat gluten is now sold on its own by some specialty flour companies (like Bob's Red Mill), so you can easily acquire it. Wheat is made up of starch and protein—the starch is stripped away, leaving just the protein, which is wheat gluten.

In this book we make a variety of different types of seitan, many of which utilize other ingredients to enhance the flavor and texture. All of the additional ingredients are easy to find and likely already live in your pantry.

Pantry

Here are some of the recommended ingredients and supplies to have on hand to turn your kitchen into a regular wheat gluten butcher's shop!

Vital wheat gluten flour: This is the basis upon which all faux meat depends. Well, seitan at least. You can get it in bulk at most co-ops and natural food stores, in addition to small bags/boxes from specialty flour companies. I recommend Bob's Red Mill or King Arthur Flour.

Chickpea flour: This is used in small amounts in this book. Buy it in bulk—a full-sized bag will last you a long while.

Store unused chickpea flour in the freezer in a well-sealed container for up to 12 months.

Spices and herbs:

- Fennel seeds
- Garlic powder
- Onion powder
- Oregano
- Pepper
- Sage
- Salt
- Soy sauce/tamari

Other food items:

- Canned beans (pinto, cannellini, navy, and black)
- Liquid smoke flavoring
- Low-sodium vegetable broth
- Nutritional yeast
- Tomato paste

Supplies:

- Cooking twine
- Cheesecloth
- Steamer insert, large (see "Cooking Seitan" page 6)
- Tin foil

Cooking Seitan

There are a several different methods for cooking seitan. While I provide specific ways for cooking each recipe, you may find that you really prefer one style over another, and I encourage you to experiment.

In Broth

The standard, tried-and-true way of preparing seitan is by simmering it in broth. This adds moisture and helps infuse it with flavor. However, in some cases, this can make the outer part of the seitan too moist, leaving you with something resembling "brains" from a horror movie more than anything you'd want to eat. In the recipes where we cook the seitan in broth by itself, I tend to use the broth just to cover it, letting it simmer rather than being completely submerged.

This is why you'll see me often adding resistance to the seitan by loosely wrapping it in cheesecloth and tying the ends off with cooking twine. This gives structure to the seitan, keeping it compact and firm, at the same time allowing it to gain the juicy benefits of the broth.

> ***Pro tip:*** Whenever you're cooking seitan in broth, lower the liquid to a simmer after adding the seitan—if it continues to boil, the broth will be too hot and the resulting seitan can be rubbery.

In Foil

Steaming: Wrapping seitan in foil and steaming it over water is a great way to prepare seitan so the wheat meat itself has more flavor, in addition to creating smaller portions. For example, take sausages and burgers. These often have beans, grains, and more robust flavor profiles, so steaming gives us the opportunity to cook them in a way that maintains that flavor while making them nice and tender. If we were to cook them in broth, the seasoning would be cooked out and diluted.

To steam seitan, I recommend buying a steamer insert for a large stock pot. This is the most versatile way of steaming and will be the easiest for you. Otherwise, you could use a large, metal vegetable steaming basket in the bottom of a pot; however, with this method you can't fit as much water in the pot, and you'll need to keep an eye on it and refill often to keep from burning the seitan or ruining your pot.

You can also try steaming seitan in a rice cooker with a steaming basket, but models vary greatly and the tin foil can get too hot for plastic inserts, so experiment at your own risk. I have had very inconsistent results from rice cookers and prefer a steamer basket in my stock pot.

Baking: This is for special circumstances, for wheat meats that are a little drier, or as a finishing technique for seitan that has been partially steamed. This results in a denser meat, one that is good for finely slicing.

> ***Pro tip:*** Whenever using foil, always double wrap the seitan. While cooking, it will expand and will sometimes tear the foil.

Storing Seitan

Freshly cooked seitan can be stored in the fridge for five to seven days after preparation (always employ the sniff test after four or five days). For seitan cooked in broth, store covered in broth. For other variations, store wrapped in foil or plastic wrap, to keep it moist.

For larger batches, you can freeze seitan, well wrapped, for up to two months. Let it defrost in the refrigerator before using.

The Basics

With these basic recipes, you'll hone your seitan skills and be provided with a broad base for preparing nearly any wheat meat dish. These recipes range in their cooking techniques, giving you experience with simmering, steaming, and baking your seitan. The finished product for most recipes is, essentially, "uncooked meat," meaning the seitan will be ready to be incorporated into a recipe, but might not be delectable on its own.

Don't let some of the lengthy ingredient lists scare you—they are just a pinch of this, a scoop of that, and almost everything will already be in your kitchen. Those little bits add up to a great flavor in the end.

This chapter is basically a playground where you get your basics down and experiment with different methods of cooking, and can then springboard into making your own creations and the more challenging recipes included in this book.

Your Grandma's Seitan

BROTH METHOD

We are lucky enough to live in an era where vital wheat gluten flour is readily available at grocery stores, making seitan a cinch to make. It hasn't always been that way, however, and sometimes you'll want to make something from homestead-style *scratch.* In the case of seitan, that means using straight-up flour and kneading and rinsing out the starch to leave our tasty gluten. You can use a mixer with a dough hook for this, but it gets very dense, so I prefer to use my hands.

Makes 4 to 5 servings

For the seitan mixture:

3 cups whole wheat flour

3 cups unbleached all-purpose flour

3 cups cool water

For the cooking broth:

8 cups water

1/3 cup soy sauce

1/4 cup tomato paste

1 onion, quartered

2 carrots, roughly chopped

5 cloves garlic, roughly crushed with the side of a knife

1. In a large bowl, combine the flours then add the water. Mix until a tough dough comes together and feels like really dense bread dough.

2. Form the dough into a small, cohesive ball, adding a tiny bit of water if needed. Cover the ball of dough completely in cold water and let sit for 1 hour.

3. Drain the dough then cover in fresh, cold water. In the water, knead the dough until the water becomes cloudy. Drain, cover in fresh water, and knead again.

4. Knead the dough until it becomes elastic and rubbery, changing the water as needed. The water might still be slightly cloudy, but you should have about 2½ cups of very dense, rubbery seitan. Divide the seitan in half.

5. Cut 2 pieces of cheesecloth long enough to loosely wrap around each seitan chunk twice, and long enough on the ends to securely tie off with some cooking twine.

6. Combine the ingredients for the broth in a large stock pot and bring to a boil. Gently drop in the seitan pieces. Reduce the heat to a simmer.

7. Cook for 40 minutes, covered, rotating each chunk of seitan halfway through. Remove from the heat and let cool in the broth for 15 minutes, uncovered, before using.

8. Seitan can be used right away (cubed, sliced, or halved and added to a recipe, or sautéed with a little olive oil). Otherwise, drain the solids from the broth and store, refrigerated and covered in broth, for up to 5 days.

Basic Seitan 2.0

BROTH METHOD

This method of basic seitan brings us into the modern era, where machines have separated out the starch from protein and we can whip up a batch of seitan faster than Granny can say, "Rinse"! This recipe makes a nicely textured batch of seitan with a neutral flavor base, great to use in recipes where you have a serious marinade or spice profile.

Makes 4 to 5 servings

For the seitan mixture:

- 1 ½ cups vital wheat gluten
- 3 tablespoons nutritional yeast
- 2 tablespoons unbleached all-purpose flour
- ¾ cup low-sodium vegetable broth
- ¼ cup soy sauce
- 2 tablespoons olive oil

For the cooking broth:

- 8 cups water
- ⅓ cup soy sauce
- ¼ cup tomato paste
- 1 onion, quartered
- 2 carrots, roughly chopped into chunks
- 5 cloves garlic, roughly crushed with the side of a knife

1. In a large bowl, combine the wheat gluten, nutritional yeast, and flour. Make a well in the dry ingredients and pour in the vegetable broth, soy sauce, and olive oil.

2. Whisk the wet ingredients into the dry and knead until well-incorporated and it comes together into a cohesive dough. The dough should feel pretty elastic and fairly smooth. Divide in half.

3. Cut 2 pieces of cheesecloth long enough to loosely wrap around each seitan chunk twice, and long enough on the ends to securely tie off with some cooking twine.

4. Combine the ingredients for the broth in a large stock pot and bring to a boil. Gently drop in the seitan pieces. Reduce heat to a simmer.

5. Cook for 40 minutes, covered, rotating each piece of seitan halfway through. Remove from the heat and let cool in broth for 15 minutes, uncovered, before using.

6. Seitan can be used right away (cubed, sliced, or halved and added to a recipe, or sautéed with a little olive oil). Otherwise, drain the solids from the broth and store, refrigerated and covered in broth, for up to 5 days.

Basic Chick'n

STEAM METHOD

Whether you want to make cutlets, top a salad with meaty chunks, or have chicken fried steak, this recipe has you covered.

Makes 4 to 6 servings

1 ½ cups vital wheat gluten

¼ cup chickpea flour

¼ cup nutritional yeast

1 teaspoon garlic powder

½ teaspoon paprika

½ teaspoon onion powder

½ teaspoon sea salt

1 cup low-sodium vegetable broth

½ cup shredded carrots

½ cup shredded onion

¼ cup soy sauce

2 tablespoons olive oil

1. Prepare 4 pieces of tin foil, large enough to wrap up each sausage well, with overhang to twist each end shut.
2. In a large bowl, combine the wheat gluten, chickpea flour, nutritional yeast, garlic powder, paprika, onion powder, and salt. In a smaller bowl, whisk together the vegetable broth, shredded carrots, onion, soy sauce, and olive oil.
3. Whisk the wet ingredients into the dry and knead until well-incorporated and it comes together into a cohesive dough. The dough should feel pretty elastic and fairly smooth.
4. Let the dough rest for a few minutes while you prepare your steamer (see page 7 for suggestions). Bring the water to a boil.
5. Divide the dough into 4 pieces and shape to resemble small loaves. Wrap in tin foil and twist the ends to secure.

6. Place in the basket of a steamer and cook for 30 minutes, covered. It's best if you can place them in a single layer, but if you have to stack them, rotate them halfway through. (Be sure to check water level and to add as needed, as it may steam itself dry.)
7. Remove the chick'n from the steamer and let rest for 15 minutes before unwrapping and using.
8. Store leftover chick'n, wrapped in tin foil, in the fridge for up to 1 week.

Variation: For cutlets, separate the dough into 6 pieces, press between 2 pieces of waxed paper, and flatten with a rolling pin. Wrap each cutlet between 2 pieces of tin foil, folding the overhanging edges of the foil tightly together, and steam for 20 minutes.

Basic Beef

BROTH METHOD

This basic recipe makes, essentially, a slab of meat. Braising the beef seitan after initially cooking is a great way to seal in moisture and add more flavor and texture, giving you a meatier experience.

Makes 4 to 5 servings

For the seitan mixture:

1 ½ cups vital wheat gluten

¼ cup nutritional yeast

2 tablespoons unbleached all-purpose flour

1 teaspoon garlic powder

½ teaspoon paprika

½ teaspoon onion powder

¼ teaspoon freshly ground pepper

1 cup low-sodium vegetable broth

½ cup shredded raw beet

½ cup shredded onion

¼ cup soy sauce

2 tablespoons olive oil

½ teaspoon molasses

½ teaspoon liquid smoke

For the cooking broth:

8 cups water

⅓ cup soy sauce

¼ cup tomato paste

1 onion, quartered

5 cloves garlic, roughly crushed with the side of a knife

1. In a large bowl, combine the wheat gluten, nutritional yeast, all-purpose flour, garlic powder, paprika, onion powder, and pepper. In a small bowl, combine the vegetable broth, beet, onion, soy sauce, olive oil, molasses, and liquid smoke.
2. Whisk the wet ingredients into the dry, and knead until well-incorporated and it comes together into a cohesive

dough. The dough should feel pretty elastic and fairly smooth. Shape into a large loaf.

3. Cut 1 large piece of cheesecloth long enough to loosely wrap around the seitan chunk twice, and long enough on the ends to securely tie off with some cooking twine.

4. Combine the ingredients for broth in a large stock pot and bring to a boil. Gently drop in the seitan. Reduce the heat to a simmer.

5. Cook for 50 minutes, covered, rotating the seitan halfway through. Remove from the heat and let cool in the broth for 15 minutes, uncovered, before using.

6. Seitan can be used right away (cubed, sliced, or halved and added to a recipe, or sautéed with a little olive oil). Otherwise, drain the solids from the broth and store, refrigerated and covered in broth, for up to 5 days.

Basic Ham

BROTH METHOD/FINISH IN OVEN

This recipe makes a lovely, pink-hued wheat ham that is perfect with a Dijon glaze. While you're at it, watch the "Queen of Jordan" episode of *30 Rock* (season 5, episode 17) to entertain you while you make this. You and your ham-eating family can thank me later.

Makes 2 small hams (6 servings)

For the seitan mixture:

- 2 cups vital wheat gluten
- 1/4 cup nutritional yeast
- 2 tablespoons unbleached all-purpose flour
- 1 teaspoon garlic powder
- 1 teaspoon paprika
- 1 teaspoon onion powder
- 1/4 teaspoon ground cloves
- 1 1/4 cups apple juice
- 3/4 cup cooked navy or cannellini beans, rinsed and drained
- 1/4 cup tomato paste
- 2 tablespoons olive oil
- 2 tablespoons soy sauce
- 1 tablespoon apple cider vinegar
- 2 teaspoons liquid smoke

For the cooking broth:

- 4 cups water
- 2 cups tomato sauce
- 2 cups pineapple juice
- 1/3 cup soy sauce
- 1/4 cup tomato paste
- 1 onion, quartered
- 5 cloves garlic, roughly crushed with the side of a knife

For the finishing glaze:

- 1/3 cup brown sugar
- 1/2 cup apple juice
- 2 tablespoons Dijon mustard
- 1 tablespoon vegetable oil

1. In a large bowl, combine the wheat gluten, nutritional yeast, all-purpose flour, garlic powder, paprika, onion powder, and cloves.
2. In the bowl of a food processor or blender, combine the apple juice, beans, tomato paste, olive oil, soy sauce, vinegar, and liquid smoke. Blend until smooth.
3. Add the dry ingredients into the wet and pulse until combined. Turn out onto a clean surface and knead until well-incorporated and it comes together into a cohesive dough. The dough should feel pretty elastic and fairly smooth. Divide in half.
4. Cut 2 pieces of cheesecloth long enough to loosely wrap around each seitan chunk twice, and long enough on the ends to securely tie off with some cooking twine.
5. Combine the ingredients for the broth in a large stock pot and bring to a boil. Gently drop in the seitan pieces. Reduce the heat to a simmer.
6. Cook for 40 minutes, covered, rotating each chunk of seitan halfway through. Remove from the heat and let cool in the broth for 15 minutes, uncovered, before removing.
7. Preheat the oven to 375°F. Line a large baking pan with parchment paper or tin foil. Spray with oil.
8. In a small bowl, combine the finishing glaze ingredients until relatively smooth.
9. Place the hams on the prepared pan and brush with glaze. Bake for 15 to 20 minutes, until bronzed to your liking, brushing on another layer of glaze halfway through.
10. Ham can be used as is, carved for a meal, or sliced into amazing lunch meat.

Basic Sausages

STEAM METHOD

Consider this a base recipe from which you can make sausages of any flavor profile or theme.

Makes 4 to 6 sausages

1 ¼ cups vital wheat gluten

2 tablespoons nutritional yeast

½ teaspoon onion powder

½ teaspoon oregano

salt and freshly ground pepper to taste

1 cup low-sodium vegetable broth

¾ cup cooked navy or cannellini beans, rinsed and drained

2 tablespoons olive oil

2 tablespoons soy sauce

2 tablespoons agave or maple syrup

1 tablespoon red wine vinegar

2 cloves garlic, peeled and roughly chopped

1. Prepare your steaming setup (see page 7 for suggestions). Bring water to a boil and cover. Ready 4 to 6 pieces of tin foil, large enough to wrap up each sausage well, with overhang to twist each end shut.
2. In a medium bowl, combine the wheat gluten, nutritional yeast, onion powder, oregano, salt, and pepper.
3. In the bowl of a food processor or blender, combine the vegetable broth, beans, olive oil, soy sauce, agave or maple syrup, red wine vinegar, and garlic. Blend until smooth.
4. Add the dry ingredients to the wet and pulse until combined. Turn out onto a clean surface and knead until smooth and elastic, 2 to 3 minutes.

5. Divide into 4 to 6 pieces (depending on how large you want your sausages). Roll each piece out between your hands and wrap up in tin foil. If the dough resists being formed, wrap the foil around it in the way you'd like it to be shaped and it will conform while cooking.
6. Place the sausages in the steamer and cook for 30 minutes, rotating them halfway through if they are not in a single layer. (Be sure to check the water level and to add water as needed, as it may steam itself dry.)
7. Let cool for 30 minutes before carefully unwrapping the sausages and using in a recipe.

Basic Lunch Meat

STEAM METHOD/FINISH IN OVEN

Sometimes you need a sammich. This basic lunch meat tastes like, well, chicken. Pile it high with your favorite fixin's and chow down!

Makes 4 to 6 servings

- 2 cups vital wheat gluten
- ¼ cup nutritional yeast
- 2 teaspoons onion powder
- 1 teaspoon garlic powder
- ½ teaspoon paprika
- 1 (15-ounce) can navy or cannellini beans, drained and rinsed
- 1 ¼ cups low-sodium vegetable broth
- 2 tablespoons olive oil
- 2 tablespoons soy sauce
- ¼ teaspoon liquid smoke

1. Prepare your steaming setup (see page 7 for suggestions). Bring water to a boil and cover.
2. Ready enough foil to wrap 1 large loaf twice, with overhang to twist each end shut.
3. In a large bowl, combine the wheat gluten, nutritional yeast, onion powder, garlic powder, and paprika.
4. In the bowl of a food processor or blender, combine the beans, vegetable broth, oil, soy sauce, and liquid smoke. Blend until smooth.
5. Add the dry ingredients to the wet and pulse to combine, then turn out onto a flat surface and knead to combine, until elastic. Shape into a large loaf-life cylinder and double wrap in tin foil, twisting the ends to secure. The loaf should be short enough to fit in your steamer.

6. Place in the basket of a steamer and cook for 50 minutes, covered. (Be sure to check the water level and to add water as needed, as it may steam itself dry.)

7. Toward the end of steaming, preheat the oven to 350°F. Remove the loaf from steamer and transfer to a baking sheet, still in the tin foil.

8. Bake for 30 minutes.

9. Remove from oven and let cool for at least an hour before unwrapping.

10. Lunch meat is best if chilled, then sliced. Store leftover lunch meat, sealed in a plastic bag or plastic wrap, in the fridge for up to a week.

Basic Burgers

PAN FRY

Fry 'em, grill 'em, pile 'em up high, or keep 'em nice and simple—it's your burger, baby!

Makes 4 to 6 servings

- 2 cups of white or cremini mushrooms, chopped
- 1 (15-ounce) can chickpeas, rinsed and drained
- 1/4 cup large-grated onion, preferably red
- 2 tablespoons olive oil
- 2 tablespoons soy sauce
- 2 cloves garlic, minced
- 1/3 cup vital wheat gluten
- 1 tablespoon nutritional yeast
- 1/2 teaspoon onion powder
- sprinkle of sea salt and freshly ground pepper

1. In a small skillet over medium heat, sauté the mushrooms until the juices are released, about 5 minutes, using a bit of oil if needed to prevent sticking.
2. Drain the liquid and transfer the mushrooms to a bowl. Add the chickpeas, onion, olive oil, soy sauce, and garlic, and mash to combine with a potato masher.
3. In a small bowl, combine the wheat gluten, nutritional yeast, onion powder, salt, and pepper. Add the dry ingredients to the wet mixture and mix with your hands, adding a tablespoon or two of water if needed, to make a hamburger-like texture. Knead slightly to incorporate everything.
4. Divide the mixture into 4 to 6 patties, depending on how thick you like your burgers.

5. Heat a skillet over medium heat with a little oil, and cook the patties until cooked through and browned on both sides, about 5 minutes per side.
6. Serve as is or baste with a little oil and throw on the grill for more flavor.

Ground Not-Beef

STEAM METHOD

This is an easy recipe that will serve you well—whether making tacos or nachos or "beefing up" your spaghetti sauce, this protein-powered ground beef alternative is a big winner.

Makes 4 to 5 servings

- 1 ½ cups vital wheat gluten
- ¼ cup chickpea flour
- ¼ cup nutritional yeast
- 1 teaspoon paprika
- ½ teaspoon onion powder
- ½ teaspoon garlic powder
- ¼ teaspoon salt
- ¼ teaspoon freshly ground pepper
- 1 cup low-sodium vegetable broth
- ¼ cup shredded onion
- ¼ cup shredded carrot
- 3 cloves garlic, crushed
- 2 tablespoons olive oil
- 2 tablespoons soy sauce
- 2 tablespoons tomato paste
- 1 teaspoon liquid smoke

1. Prepare your steaming setup (see page 7 for suggestions). Bring water to a boil and cover.
2. Ready enough foil to wrap 1 large loaf twice, with overhang to twist each end shut.
3. In a large bowl, combine the wheat gluten, chickpea flour, nutritional yeast, paprika, onion powder, garlic powder, salt, and pepper.
4. In a medium bowl, whisk together the vegetable broth, shredded onion and carrot, garlic, olive oil, soy sauce, tomato paste, and liquid smoke.

5. Add the wet ingredients to the dry and mix together, kneading with your hands until smooth and combined. Shape into a large loaf-life cylinder and double wrap in tin foil, twisting the ends to secure. The loaf should be short enough to fit in your steamer.
6. Place in the basket of a steamer and cook for 50 minutes, covered. (Be sure to check the water level and to add water as needed, as it may steam itself dry.)
7. Let cool completely before unwrapped and shredding or grating—you can pulse in your food processor or use a cheese grater. Add a little drizzle of oil or vegetable broth to moisten and get the meat to hold together.
8. Use in a recipe of your choice in place of ground beef. Store in an airtight bag in the fridge for up to a week.

The Next Level

You've mastered the basics, so now we'll up the ante with more layered seitan recipes and options to take your faux meat–making skills to the next level.

Chick'n Wings

STEAM METHOD

This recipe is everything you need to make chicken wings of all kinds—sautéed, marinated, breaded, stir-fried. However you cook 'em, they're tasty!

Makes 4 to 6 servings

- 1 ½ cups vital wheat gluten
- ¼ cup chickpea flour
- ¼ cup nutritional yeast
- 1 teaspoon garlic powder
- 1 teaspoon onion powder
- ½ teaspoon paprika
- ½ teaspoon sea salt
- 1 cup low-sodium vegetable broth
- ½ cup shredded onion
- ¼ cup soy sauce
- 2 tablespoons tomato paste
- 2 tablespoons olive oil

1. Ready 12 pieces of tin foil, large enough to wrap up each chick'n wing well, with overhang to twist each end shut.
2. In a large bowl, combine the wheat gluten, chickpea flour, nutritional yeast, garlic powder, onion powder, paprika, and salt. In a smaller bowl, whisk together the vegetable broth, onion, soy sauce, tomato paste, and olive oil.
3. Whisk the wet ingredients into the dry, and knead until well-incorporated and it comes together into a cohesive dough. The dough should feel pretty elastic and fairly smooth.
4. Let the dough rest for a few minutes while you prepare your steaming setup (see page 6 for suggestions). Bring water to a boil and cover.

5. Divide the dough into 4 pieces, then each of those into 3 smaller pieces, to resemble chicken wings. Wrap in tin foil and twist ends to secure. Place a plate on top of them and weigh it down to help them flatten slightly.

6. Place in the basket of the steamer and cook for 25 minutes, covered. If you can place them in a single layer, that's ideal. If you have to stack them, rotate them halfway through. (Be sure to check the water level and to add water as needed, as it may steam itself dry.)

7. Remove from steamer and let rest for 15 minutes before unwrapping and using.

8. Store leftover chick'n wings, wrapped in tin foil, in fridge for up to a week.

Ribs or No-Beef Tips

BROTH METHOD

As written, this recipe makes some tasty ribs. For beef tips, cook as directed, then cut each strip into 4 pieces before searing in step 8.

Makes 4 to 5 servings

For the seitan mixture:

- 1 ½ cups vital wheat gluten
- ¼ cup nutritional yeast
- 2 tablespoons unbleached all-purpose flour
- 1 teaspoon garlic powder
- ½ teaspoon paprika
- ½ teaspoon onion powder
- ¼ teaspoon freshly ground pepper
- 1 cup low-sodium vegetable broth
- ½ cup shredded raw beet
- ½ cup shredded onion
- ¼ cup soy sauce
- 2 tablespoons olive oil
- ½ teaspoon molasses
- ½ teaspoon liquid smoke

For the cooking broth:

- 8 cups water
- ⅓ cup soy sauce
- ¼ cup tomato paste
- 1 onion, quartered
- 5 cloves garlic, roughly crushed with the side of a knife

For the searing ingredients:

- ¼ cup cornstarch
- vegetable or canola oil
- a little red wine, vermouth, or vegetable stock

1. In a large bowl, combine the wheat gluten, nutritional yeast, flour, garlic powder, paprika, onion powder, and pepper. In a small bowl, combine the vegetable broth,

beet, onion, soy sauce, olive oil, molasses, and liquid smoke.

2. Whisk the wet ingredients into the dry, and knead until well-incorporated and it comes together into a cohesive dough. The dough should feel pretty elastic and fairly smooth.

3. Cut the dough in half. Divide each half twice, cutting the long way, so you end up with 8 long slices total.

4. Cut 8 pieces of cheesecloth long enough to loosely wrap around each seitan chunk twice, and long enough on the ends to securely tie off with some cooking twine.

5. Combine the ingredients for the broth in a large stock pot and bring to a boil. Gently drop in the seitan pieces. Reduce the heat to a simmer.

6. Cook for 25 minutes, covered, flipping the seitan halfway through. Remove from the heat and let sit in the broth for 15 minutes, uncovered, before removing to cool until it's cool enough to touch.

7. Sprinkle the ribs with cornstarch. (Alternatively, you can put the cornstarch in a large bag, add the ribs, and gently toss, but you want the coating to be light).

8. Heat a thin layer of oil over medium-high heat in a skillet until it gently sizzles when you sprinkle a droplet of water in it (careful!). Add the ribs in one layer, with a little space between each one. Cook until they are browned on one side, 3 to 5 minutes, before flipping to the other side. Add a little wine, vermouth, or vegetable stock as needed to help keep them from sticking to the bottom. I normally only sear 2 of the 4 sides of the ribs,

so they have a more complex texture, but you can sear all 4 sides if you want.

9. Serve as is, add to a recipe, or top with a sauce before serving.

Italian Sausages

STEAM METHOD

Chop them up and add to pasta dishes, or throw them in a bun—these tasty sausages are flavorful and delicious!

Makes 4 to 6 sausages

- 1 1/4 cups vital wheat gluten
- 2 tablespoons nutritional yeast
- 1 teaspoon dried oregano
- 1 teaspoon dried basil
- 1 teaspoon paprika
- 1 teaspoon crushed fennel seeds
- 1/2 teaspoon red pepper flakes (if you want it spicier)
- sprinkle of sea salt and freshly ground pepper
- 1 cup low-sodium vegetable broth
- 3/4 cup cooked navy or cannellini beans, rinsed and drained
- 2 tablespoons olive oil
- 2 tablespoons soy sauce
- 2 tablespoons tomato paste
- 1 tablespoon maple syrup or agave
- 2 cloves garlic, roughly chopped

1. Prepare your steaming setup (see page 7 for suggestions). Bring water to a boil and cover. Ready 4 to 6 pieces of tin foil, large enough to wrap up each sausage well, with overhang to twist each end shut.
2. In a bowl, combine the wheat gluten, nutritional yeast, oregano, basil, paprika, fennel seeds, red pepper flakes, sea salt, and freshly ground pepper.
3. In the bowl of a food processor or blender, combine the vegetable broth, beans, olive oil, soy sauce, tomato paste, maple syrup or agave, and garlic. Blend until smooth.

4. Add the dry ingredients and pulse until combined. Turn out onto a clean surface and knead until smooth and elastic, 2 to 3 minutes.
5. Divide into 4 to 6 pieces (depending on how large you want your sausages). Roll each piece out between your hands and wrap up in tin foil. If the dough resists being formed, wrap the foil around it in the way you'd like it to be shaped and it will conform while cooking.
6. Place the sausages in the steamer and cook for 30 minutes, rotating them halfway through if they are not in a single layer. (Be sure to check the water level and to add water as needed, as it may steam itself dry.)
7. Let cool for 30 minutes before carefully unwrapping the sausages and using in a recipe.

Mexican Sausages

STEAM METHOD

Yum! Slice into a tortilla, add to your breakfast scramble, or chop up for tacos.

Makes 4 to 6 sausages

- 1 1/4 cups vital wheat gluten
- 2 tablespoons nutritional yeast
- 1 tablespoon dried chili powder (ancho, if available)
- 1 teaspoon ground cumin
- 1 teaspoon ground coriander
- 1/8 to 1/4 teaspoon cayenne pepper
- salt and freshly ground pepper to taste
- 1 cup low-sodium vegetable broth
- 3/4 cup cooked pinto beans, rinsed and drained
- 2 tablespoons olive oil
- 2 tablespoons soy sauce
- 2 tablespoons tomato paste
- 1 tablespoon maple syrup or agave
- 2 cloves garlic, roughly chopped

1. Prep your steaming setup (see page 7 for suggestions). Bring water to a boil and cover. Ready 4 to 6 pieces of tin foil, large enough to wrap up each sausage well, with overhang to twist each end shut.

2. In a bowl, combine the wheat gluten, nutritional yeast, chili powder, cumin, coriander, cayenne as desired for spiciness, salt, and pepper.

3. In the bowl of a food processor or blender, combine the vegetable broth, beans, olive oil, soy sauce, tomato paste, maple syrup or agave, and garlic. Blend until smooth.

4. Add the dry ingredients and pulse until combined. Turn out onto a clean surface and knead until smooth and elastic, 2 to 3 minutes.

5. Divide into 4 to 6 pieces (depending on how large you want your sausages). Roll each piece out between your hands and wrap up in tin foil. If the dough resists being formed, wrap the foil around it in the way you'd like it to be shaped and it will conform while cooking.

6. Place the sausages in the steamer and cook for 30 minutes, rotating them halfway through if they are not in a single layer. (Be sure to check the water level and to add water as needed, as it may steam itself dry.)

7. Let cool for 30 minutes before carefully unwrapping and using in a recipe.

Kielbasa

STEAM METHOD

I'd really be disrespecting my Polish heritage if I didn't include some kielbasa in here. All of the flavor, none of the guilt!

Makes 4 to 6 sausages

- 1¼ cups vital wheat gluten
- 2 tablespoons nutritional yeast
- 2 tablespoons brown sugar
- 1 teaspoon paprika
- 1 teaspoon dried marjoram
- ¾ teaspoon ground fennel
- ½ teaspoon red pepper flakes (optional)
- salt and freshly ground pepper to taste
- 1 cup low-sodium vegetable broth
- ¾ cup cooked kidney beans, rinsed and drained
- 2 tablespoons olive oil
- 2 tablespoons soy sauce
- 1 tablespoon red wine vinegar
- 1 tablespoon tomato paste
- 1 teaspoon liquid smoke
- 2 cloves garlic, roughly chopped

1. Prep your steaming setup (see page 7 for suggestions). Bring water to a boil and cover. Ready 4 to 6 pieces of tin foil, large enough to wrap up each sausage well, with overhang to twist each end shut.

2. In a bowl, combine the wheat gluten, nutritional yeast, brown sugar, paprika, marjoram, fennel, red pepper flakes (if using), salt, and pepper.

3. In the bowl of a food processor or blender, combine the vegetable broth, beans, olive oil, soy sauce, vinegar, tomato paste, liquid smoke, and garlic. Blend until smooth.

4. Add the dry ingredients and pulse until combined. Turn out onto a clean surface and knead until smooth and elastic, 2 to 3 minutes.

5. Divide into 4 to 6 pieces (depending on how large you want your sausages). Roll each piece out between your hands and wrap up in tin foil. If the dough resists being formed, wrap the foil around it in the way you'd like it to be shaped and it will conform while cooking.

6. Place the sausages in the steamer and cook for 30 minutes, rotating them halfway through if they are not in a single layer. (Be sure to check the water level and to add water as needed, as it may steam itself dry.)

7. Let cool for 30 minutes before carefully unwrapping and using in a recipe.

Beer Brats

STEAM METHOD

Summer is not summer until you've pulled out the grill. Baste these bad boys with a little oil and throw them on to the delight of all of your guests.

Makes 4 to 6 sausages

- 1 1/4 cups vital wheat gluten
- 2 tablespoons nutritional yeast
- 1/2 teaspoon dried, ground marjoram
- 1/2 teaspoon celery salt
- 1/2 teaspoon onion powder
- 1/4 teaspoon ground allspice
- salt and freshly ground pepper to taste
- 1 cup beer (like an IPA)
- 3/4 cup cooked pinto beans, rinsed and drained
- 3 tablespoons chopped fresh parsley
- 2 tablespoons olive oil
- 2 tablespoons soy sauce
- 2 tablespoons soy sauce
- 1 tablespoon agave or maple syrup
- 2 cloves garlic, roughly chopped

1. Prep your steaming setup (see page 7 for suggestions). Bring water to a boil and cover. Ready 4 to 6 pieces of tin foil, large enough to wrap up each sausage well, with overhang to twist each end shut.
2. In a bowl, combine the wheat gluten, nutritional yeast, marjoram, celery salt, onion powder, allspice, salt, and pepper.
3. In the bowl of a food processor or blender, combine the beer, beans, parsley, olive oil, soy sauce, agave or maple syrup, and garlic. Blend until smooth.

4. Add the dry ingredients and pulse until combined. Turn out onto a clean surface and knead until smooth and elastic, 2 to 3 minutes.
5. Divide into 4 to 6 pieces (depending on how large you want your sausages). Roll each piece out between your hands and wrap up in tin foil. If the dough resists being formed, wrap the foil around it in the way you'd like it to be shaped and it will conform while cooking.
6. Place the sausages in the steamer and cook for 30 minutes, rotating them halfway through if they are not in a single layer. (Be sure to check the water level and to add water as needed, as it may steam itself dry.)
7. Let cool for 30 minutes before carefully unwrapping and using in a recipe. Or try grilling them!

Seitan Fakin' Bacon

BAKED METHOD

This seitan recipe takes it all the way—layering pink and white layers of seitan to make "marbled," smoky fakin' "bacon" that you can use to layer on a sandwich, crumble on a salad, or just eat mindlessly while standing in your kitchen in your underwear, staring into space while trying to figure out what you're doing for the day. There's no shame in fakin'.

Makes 4 to 5 servings

For the pink dough:

- 1 cup vital wheat gluten
- 2 tablespoons chickpea flour
- 1 teaspoon garlic powder
- 1 teaspoon onion powder
- 1 teaspoon smoked paprika
- salt and freshly ground pepper to taste
- ½ cup water
- 2 tablespoons tomato paste
- 2 tablespoons soy sauce
- 1 tablespoon olive oil
- 2 tablespoons maple syrup, divided
- 3 teaspoons liquid smoke, divided

For the white dough:

- ½ cup vital wheat gluten
- 1 tablespoon chickpea flour
- ¼ teaspoon garlic powder
- ½ teaspoon onion powder
- ⅓ cup water
- 1 teaspoon olive oil

1. For the pink dough, in a large bowl, whisk together the wheat gluten, chickpea flour, garlic powder, onion powder, paprika, salt, and pepper.

2. In a medium bowl, whisk together the water for the pink dough, tomato paste, soy sauce, olive oil, 1 tablespoon of maple syrup, and 2 teaspoons of liquid smoke. Whisk to combine.
3. Add the wet ingredients to the dry and mix to combine. Mix well, until everything comes together.
4. Combine the remaining maple syrup and liquid smoke in a small bowl and set aside.
5. For the white dough, in a medium bowl, whisk together the wheat gluten, chickpea flour, garlic powder, onion powder, salt, and pepper.
6. Reusing the wet bowl, whisk together the water for the white dough and the olive oil. Add the wet ingredients to the dry and mix to combine.
7. Divide each piece of dough in half. Roll out half of the white dough into a thin square, about 8 x 8 inches, and place on a large sheet of tin foil.
8. Roll out half of the pink dough to similar dimensions and place on top of white dough. Repeat with the remaining dough.
9. Top with a sheet of tin foil and place a cutting board on top. Weigh down with a heavy book and let sit for 30 minutes, to set the shape.
10. Preheat the oven to 325°F. Remove the book and cutting board from seitan and lift up the top piece of tin foil.
11. Gently whisk together the reserved maple syrup and liquid smoke, and brush the top and sides of the seitan with it. Add a sprinkle of freshly ground pepper. Replace

the top piece of tin foil and roll the edges of the top and bottom of the tin foil to enclose the seitan.

12. Transfer to a baking sheet and bake for 45 minutes, flipping halfway through baking. Let cool for 30 minutes before removing from the foil. Slice into ¼- to ½-inch-thick slices.

13. This seitan will be slightly soft, which is perfect for slicing and frying or incorporating into other recipes.

Smoky Maple Breakfast Links

STEAM METHOD

These are seriously tasty little links—sweet and smoky—that are sure to improve any breakfast or brunch plate.

Makes 8 to 10 sausages

- 1 1/4 cups vital wheat gluten
- 2 tablespoons nutritional yeast
- 2 tablespoons brown sugar
- 1 teaspoon ground sage
- 1/2 teaspoon dried, ground marjoram
- salt and freshly ground pepper to taste
- 1 cup low-sodium vegetable broth
- 1/3 cup chunky unsweetened applesauce
- 2 tablespoons olive oil
- 2 tablespoons soy sauce
- 2 tablespoons maple syrup
- 1 1/2 teaspoons liquid smoke
- 1 clove garlic, roughly chopped

1. Prepare your steaming setup (see page 7 for suggestions). Bring water to a boil and cover. Ready 8 to 10 pieces of tin foil, large enough to wrap up each sausage well, with overhang to twist each end shut.
2. In a bowl, combine the wheat gluten, nutritional yeast, brown sugar, sage, marjoram, salt, and pepper.
3. In the bowl of a food processor or blender, combine the vegetable broth, applesauce, olive oil, soy sauce, maple syrup, liquid smoke, and garlic. Blend until smooth.
4. Add the dry ingredients and pulse until combined. Turn out onto a clean surface and knead until smooth and elastic, 2 to 3 minutes.

5. Divide into 8 to 10 pieces (depending on how large you want your sausages). Roll each piece out between your hands and wrap up in tin foil. If the dough resists being formed, wrap the foil around it in the way you'd like it to be shaped and it will conform while cooking.
6. Place the sausages in the steamer and cook for 25 minutes, rotating them halfway through if they are not in a single layer. (Be sure to check the water level and to add water as needed, as it may steam itself dry.)
7. Let cool for 20 minutes before carefully unwrapping and using in a recipe.

Meaty-Spheres

STEAM METHOD

The seitan answer to meatballs, these guys take a little work to prep—wrapping each one in tin foil—but it's totally worth the time. Your efforts will be rewarded with tender, moist, and tasty meatballs, for all your meaty-sphere needs.

Makes 25 to 30 meatballs

1 ½ cups vital wheat gluten

¼ cup nutritional yeast

1 teaspoon dried oregano

1 teaspoon dried basil

1 teaspoon paprika

½ teaspoon crushed fennel seeds

¼ teaspoon red pepper flakes (optional)

1 cup low-sodium vegetable broth

½ cup shredded onion

¼ cup soy sauce

2 tablespoons olive oil

1 tablespoon tomato paste

1 tablespoon molasses

1 teaspoon liquid smoke

1. Prep your steaming setup (see page 7 for suggestions). Bring water to a boil and cover. Ready some 3 x 3-inch square pieces of tin foil, large enough to wrap up each meatball in, with overhang to twist the top shut.

2. In a large bowl, combine the wheat gluten, nutritional yeast, oregano, basil, paprika, fennel, and red pepper flakes, if using. In a small bowl, combine the vegetable broth, onion, soy sauce, olive oil, tomato paste, molasses, and liquid smoke.

3. Whisk the wet ingredients into the dry and knead until well-incorporated and it comes together into a cohesive dough. The dough should feel pretty elastic and fairly smooth.

4. Cut the dough into quarters. Halve each quarter. Depending on how big you want your meatballs to be, divide each piece into thirds or quarter them. Gently roll each chunk between your hands to round the edges.

5. Wrap each ball in a square of tin foil and twist well to secure the ends.

6. Place the meaty-spheres in the steamer and cook for 25 minutes, rotating them halfway through if they are not in a single layer. (Be sure to check the water level and to add water as needed, as it may steam itself dry.)

7. Let cool for 20 minutes before carefully unwrapping and using in a recipe.

Nutty Rice Burgers

PAN FRY

These tasty burgers are truly sublime. Chewy wild rice and slivers of almonds come together in a toothsome burger that is as delicious as it is healthy!

Makes 4 to 6 servings

½ cup uncooked wild rice

1 cup white or cremini mushrooms, chopped

1 cup cooked cannellini or navy beans, drained and rinsed

3 tablespoons slivered almonds, roughly chopped

¼ cup large grated onion (preferably red)

2 tablespoons olive oil

2 tablespoons soy sauce

2 tablespoons water

2 cloves garlic, minced

½ cup vital wheat gluten

1 tablespoon nutritional yeast

½ teaspoon onion powder

sprinkle of salt and freshly ground pepper

1. Cook the wild rice in water according to the package directions until tender. Drain any excess water and measure out 1 cup of cooked rice. Set aside to cool.

2. In a small skillet over medium heat, sauté the mushrooms until the juices are released, using a bit of oil if needed to prevent sticking.

3. Drain the mushroom liquid and transfer the mushrooms to a bowl. Add the beans, almonds, onion, olive oil, soy sauce, water, and garlic, and mash to combine with a potato masher.

4. In a small bowl, combine the wheat gluten, nutritional yeast, onion powder, salt, and pepper. Add to the wet

mixture, then add the cooked rice and mix with your hands, adding an additional tablespoon or two of water if needed, to make a hamburger-like texture. Knead slightly to incorporate everything.

5. Divide the mixture into 4 to 6 patties, depending on how thick you like your burgers.
6. Heat a skillet with a little oil on medium and cook the patties until browned on both sides and cooked through, about 5 minutes per side.
7. Serve as is or baste with a little oil and throw on the grill for more flavor.

Sausage of the Summer

BAKED

My family is of Polish descent, so cheese, crackers, sausage, pickles, and other assorted old-world amuse-bouches have always been the foundation of any family event.

This was the first seitan recipe I ever developed, inspired by the famous "Seitan O' Greatness"—the recipe featured on the Post Punk Kitchen forums in the mid-aughts, that changed homemade fake meat forever. This recipe brought summer sausage back into my life and helped me connect to those beloved memories.

This sausage is actually baked—baking makes a firmer, drier meat, perfect for a summer sausage, but not ideal for most faux meats.

Makes 1 large summer sausage

- 1 ½ cups vital wheat gluten
- 2 teaspoons paprika
- 1 teaspoon dried oregano
- 1 teaspoon fennel seeds, gently crushed
- ½ teaspoon salt
- ½ teaspoon freshly ground pepper
- ½ teaspoon mustard powder
- ½ teaspoon onion powder
- ½ teaspoon garlic powder
- ¾ cup low-sodium vegetable broth
- 3 tablespoons tomato paste
- 3 tablespoons olive oil
- 3 tablespoons soy sauce
- 1 teaspoon mild, light-colored miso
- 2 cloves garlic, crushed

1. Preheat oven to 325°F. Lay out 2 full-sized sheets of tin foil, about 16 inches long, on top of each other on the counter.

2. In a large bowl, combine the wheat gluten, paprika, oregano, fennel, salt, pepper, mustard powder, onion powder, and garlic powder, and whisk to combine.
3. In a medium bowl, whisk together the vegetable broth, tomato paste, olive oil, soy sauce, miso, and garlic. Add to the dry ingredients and mix to combine. Don't be afraid to get in there with your hands.
4. Shape into a large log, about 8 to 10 inches long, on top of the tin foil. Wrap well in the top piece of foil, gently twisting the ends and repeat with the second piece over it. (Don't twist too tight, as the sausage will expand a little as it bakes, and when twisted too firmly it will tear through the foil and shoot across the oven like a little meat cannon—which is loud and scary.)
5. Place the wrapped log directly onto the oven rack and bake for 80 to 90 minutes. The sausage should feel firm in the middle when poked with the end of a spoon. If it's still really squishy, let it continue to bake in additional 5-minute increments, no longer than 1½ hours.
6. Remove from the oven and let cool completely before unwrapping and serving. The sausage tastes best if made the day before and chilled in the fridge for a more developed flavor. Serve with crackers, mustard, and other tasty accompaniments.
7. Store sausage wrapped in plastic wrap or tin foil in refrigerator for up to a week.

Nibbles and Bites

You'll be the most popular person at the party when you show up with one of the delights contained in this tasty chapter. Or keep them for yourself and be the most popular person in your living room—no judgment.

Basic Wingz with Easy BBQ Sauce

Wings are always a treat—when the chickens live happily ever after! This basic recipe can be eaten as is or get slathered in a sauce—I include my favorite barbecue sauce for your enjoyment.

Makes 5 to 6 servings

- 1/3 cup unbleached all-purpose flour
- 1/4 teaspoon salt
- 1/4 teaspoon freshly ground pepper
- 1/4 teaspoon paprika
- 1/4 teaspoon garlic powder
- 1/4 teaspoon onion powder
- 1 recipe Chick'n Wings (page 29)
- 1/4 to 1/3 cup canola or vegetable oil
- Easy BBQ Sauce (recipe follows)

1. In a large zip-top bag or small brown paper lunch bag, combine the flour, salt, pepper, paprika, garlic powder, and onion powder, and shake to combine.

2. Drop in several Chick'n Wings and shake to coat. Set on a plate until ready to use. Repeat as needed, until all wings are coated.

3. Heat the oil in a large skillet over medium heat until the oil is hot. Use as much oil as needed to make a thin, solid coating on the bottom of the pan.

4. Carefully place the coated Chick'n Wings in a single layer, with a little bit of space between them, in the hot oil and cook for 2 to 3 minutes on each side, until golden. Remove from the pan and transfer to a plate lined with paper towels to drain. Repeat until all the wings have been cooked.

5. Serve plain, with Easy BBQ sauce, or with the sauce of your choice.

Easy BBQ Sauce

This sauce is a great base for many reasons, least of all the fact that it is a great base from which you can experiment and create variations: smokier, tangier, spicier—whatever tickles your fancy.

Makes 2½ cups

1 (15-ounce) can tomato sauce

⅓ cup apple cider vinegar

⅓ cup honey or agave

3 tablespoons tomato paste

1 tablespoon molasses

¼ cup brown sugar

2 teaspoons liquid smoke

1 teaspoon smoked paprika

1 teaspoon garlic powder

½ teaspoon onion powder

½ teaspoon freshly ground pepper

½ teaspoon salt

1. In a medium saucepan, whisk together all of the ingredients. Bring mixture to a light boil over medium-high heat. Reduce the heat to low and allow the sauce to simmer, whisking often, until slightly thickened and the flavor has melded, about 20 to 30 minutes.

2. Store in a covered container in the refrigerator for up to a week.

Buffalo Wingz with Perfect Ranch Dipping Sauce

These buffalo wings are baked, adding even more health factor to this updated version—no meat, less grease, all flavor. Adjust the spiciness to your preferred level and enjoy with Perfect Ranch Dipping Sauce, some celery and carrot sticks, and your favorite beer to wash it all down.

Makes 5 to 6 servings

- 1 cup unbleached all-purpose flour
- 1 teaspoon garlic powder
- 1 teaspoon paprika
- ¼ to ½ teaspoon cayenne pepper (optional)
- ¼ teaspoon salt
- ¼ teaspoon freshly ground pepper
- 1 cup non-dairy milk (unsweetened is best)
- 1 recipe Chick'n Wings (page 29)
- 3 tablespoons unsalted butter
- ¾ cup cayenne pepper hot sauce (I love Frank's RedHot)
- Perfect Ranch Dipping Sauce (recipe follows)

1. Preheat the oven to 450°F. If you have an oven-safe cooling rack, place on top of a rimmed baking sheet. Otherwise, a sheet of parchment paper is a good helper.
2. In a bowl, combine the flour, garlic powder, paprika, cayenne, if using, salt, and pepper, and whisk to combine. Add the milk and whisk until a thin batter comes together.
3. Dip each Chick'n Wing in the batter, coating well, then place on the prepared baking sheet (on the rack, if using). Repeat, leaving a little space between them.

4. Bake for 15 to 20 minutes, until the batter is set and slightly golden, flipping halfway through. While the Chick'n is baking, melt the butter and whisk together with the hot sauce.

5. Carefully remove the wings from the baking sheet and dip in the pepper sauce, returning to cookie sheet. Bake for 15 to 20 more minutes, flipping halfway (drizzle extra sauce on them after flipping if the sauce sticks to pan). They should look a little dark on the edges.

6. Remove and serve immediately with Perfect Ranch Dipping Sauce and crudités.

Perfect Ranch Dipping Sauce

Makes 1½ cups

½ cup mayonnaise

1 cup sour cream

2 tablespoons fresh chopped chives

½ teaspoon dried parsley

½ teaspoon dried dill

¼ teaspoon garlic powder

¼ teaspoon onion powder

⅛ teaspoon dried basil

⅛ teaspoon freshly ground pepper

⅛ teaspoon salt

1. In a small bowl, combine the mayonnaise and sour cream. Add the herbs and spices and mix until well incorporated. Let it sit in the fridge for at least 30 minutes before using to let the flavors meld.

Variation: Reduce the mayonnaise to ¼ cup and thin with a little milk to use as a dressing.

Vegan variation: Replace the mayonnaise, butter, and sour cream with non-dairy alternatives.

Jellied Crockpot "Meat"-Balls

This is a total guilty pleasure recipe—the ingredients are absurd, but the taste is delicious. Barely constituting a recipe, this dish is a popular potluck request. Don't be afraid to scale up and make a double—or even triple—batch. Crusty bread serves as a tool to sop up all of the tasty sauce.

Makes 5 to 7 servings

- 1 to 2 tablespoons vegetable oil
- 1 recipe Meaty-Spheres (page 47)
- 16 ounces grape jelly
- 1 (12-ounce) bottle cocktail sauce
- crusty bread, to serve

1. In a skillet over medium heat, heat the oil and cook the meatballs, stirring often, until slightly browned. Remove from the heat.
2. In a slow cooker, mix the jelly and cocktail sauce. It might be a little chunky, but will melt as it cooks. Add the meatballs and stir to cover. Cook on low for 2 to 3 hours before serving with crusty bread.

Lettuce Wraps with Spicy Peanut Sauce

The perfect appetizer or light dinner on warm summer days, these lettuce wraps are delicious with beef or chicken seitan.

Makes 10 to 12 wraps, depending on size

- 1 recipe Basic Chick'n (page 14) or Basic Beef (page 16)
- 1 tablespoon mild vegetable oil
- 2 teaspoons toasted sesame oil
- 1 teaspoon grated fresh ginger
- 2 cloves garlic, minced
- 3 tablespoons soy sauce
- 1 tablespoon rice wine vinegar
- 2 teaspoons sugar
- 10 to 12 Bibb lettuce leaves, rinsed and dried
- 1 cup matchstick-cut cucumbers
- 1 cup matchstick-cut carrots
- 1 cup bean sprouts
- ½ cup cilantro leaves
- 1 recipe Spicy Peanut Sauce (recipe follows)

1. Finely chop the seitan into small chunks.
2. In a large skillet, heat the vegetable oil over medium heat. Add the sesame oil and seitan and stir to coat. Cook, stirring often, until the edges of the seitan start to lightly crisp, about 2 to 3 minutes.
3. Add the ginger and garlic, stirring frequently, and cook until fragrant, about 2 minutes.
4. In a small bowl, combine the soy sauce, rice wine vinegar, and sugar, and whisk to combine. Drizzle over the seitan

and stir well to combine. Cook for 2 to 3 more minutes, until the liquid is absorbed. Remove from the heat.

5. Serve the seitan on a platter with lettuce leaves, cucumbers, carrots, bean sprouts, cilantro, and Spicy Peanut Sauce. Assemble wraps using the lettuce to contain the fillings and have folks build their own flavor combinations. Dip wraps in the sauce.

Spicy Peanut Sauce

You can also serve with Spicy Peanut Noodles (page 148).

Makes 1 cup

- 2 teaspoons mild vegetable oil
- 1 tablespoon minced shallot
- 1 teaspoon minced fresh ginger
- 1/3 cup water
- 1/4 cup soy sauce
- 2 tablespoons creamy, natural, unsalted peanut butter
- 1 teaspoon brown sugar
- 1/8 to 1/4 teaspoon red pepper flakes, as desired
- 1/2 teaspoon sriracha (optional)
- 1 tablespoon fresh lime juice

1. In a medium saucepan, heat the oil over medium heat. Sauté the shallot and ginger until fragrant, about 2 minutes.
2. Add the water, soy sauce, peanut butter, and sugar, and whisk to combine.
3. Bring to a low boil then lower heat to a simmer and add the red pepper flakes and sriracha, if using, whisking

often, until the sugar is dissolved and the peanut butter is incorporated.

4. Remove from heat and add the lime juice, whisking to combine.

Loaded Mashed Potato Balls

These are appetizer decadence. Crisp on the outside, creamy and flavorful in the middle, they are studded with fragrant chives, smoky fake bacon, and tasty cheese—the perfect appetizer. Serve with Perfect Ranch Dipping Sauce (page 57) for the ultimate indulgence.

Makes 18 to 24 pieces

- 2 teaspoons olive oil
- 3 slices Seitan Fakin' Bacon (page 42)
- 3 cups cooled plain mashed potatoes
- 1 cup shredded sharp cheddar cheese
- ¼ cup chives, chopped
- sprinkle of salt and freshly ground pepper
- ½ teaspoon garlic powder
- ½ teaspoon onion powder
- splash of milk
- 1 egg, whisked
- 2 large eggs, beaten
- ½ cup unbleached all-purpose flour
- 1 ¼ cup panko bread crumbs
- Perfect Ranch Dipping Sauce (page 57), to serve

1. Preheat the oven to 400°F. Line a large baking sheet with parchment paper and set aside.

2. In a large skillet, heat the oil over medium heat. Cook the Fakin' until lightly browned on the edges, about 2 minutes on each side. Remove from the heat to cool, then chop into small bits.

3. In a large bowl, combine the mashed potatoes, cheddar cheese, chives, chopped Fakin', a sprinkle of salt and pepper, garlic powder, and onion powder. Stir to

combine. If the potatoes are really starchy, add a splash of milk to help the mixture stick together better.

4. Prepare several small bowls: one with the beaten eggs, one with the flour, and one with the panko.

5. Place the prepared baking sheet nearby. Using a 2-tablespoon-size cookie scoop, scoop out the mashed potato mixture. Roll between your hands. Dip in flour, then dip in egg, then panko crumbs. Set on the prepared pan. Repeat with remaining mashed potato mixture.

6. Bake for 5 to 10 minutes or until golden brown.

7. Serve with Perfect Ranch Dipping Sauce.

Vegan variation: For the potato filling, replace the cheddar with 1 tablespoon mild yellow miso and 2 tablespoons nutritional yeast. You might need a splash of non-dairy milk. For the coating, replace the eggs with 1 tablespoon ground flaxseed whisked in ⅓ cup water. Let the flax mixture sit for 15 minutes before using, so it gets thick and will coat the mashed potato balls.

Potluck Sushi (aka Cream Cheese Roll-ups)

Cream cheese rolls-ups are as commonplace in the Midwest as tater tot hotdish, and in my formative years I used to avoid them. Yet after years of being meat free, I began to miss them. Here, we take them up a notch and serve them with Perfect Ranch Dipping Sauce (page 57), elevating them to a whole new level.

Makes 5 to 7 servings

- 1 (8-ounce) container cream cheese
- 1/4 teaspoon onion powder
- 1/4 teaspoon garlic powder
- 1/4 teaspoon dried dill
- salt and freshly ground pepper to taste
- 4 large flour tortillas
- 1/2 recipe Basic Lunch Meat (page 22), thinly sliced
- 1 large peeled cucumber, thinly sliced into strips with a vegetable peeler
- 1 1/3 cups shredded cheddar cheese
- 1 recipe Perfect Ranch Dipping Sauce (page 57)

1. In a small bowl, combine the cream cheese, onion powder, garlic powder, dill, and salt and pepper until smooth.
2. Spread over one side of each tortilla, up to 1/4 inch from the edge.
3. Place one layer of Basic Lunch Meat, one layer of thinly sliced cucumber, and 1/3 cup shredded cheese on top of each tortilla, keeping the layers nice and thin.

4. Wrap each tortilla tightly in a long cylinder and chill for 30 minutes to set before cutting into slices. Keep chilled until serving.

5. Serve with Perfect Ranch Dipping Sauce. You might want to thin the sauce out a little, depending on your preference.

Variation: Replace the cucumber slices with long, thin sandwich slices of pickles.

Vegan variation: Replace the cream cheese with a non-dairy version. Replace the shredded cheese with a non-dairy version or omit.

Ultimate 7-Layer Dip

There are few things in the world that I am truly vulnerable to. The perfect chewy brownie. Perfectly ripened mango. And 7-Layer Dip. I like the added kick from the chorizo spices, but if serving kids, opt for Ground Not-Beef (page 26) with some mild taco seasonings. You can always use canned refried beans, but it doesn't take long to whip up this more flavorful variation.

Makes 5 to 7 servings

- 1 to 2 tablespoons olive oil
- 1 recipe Ground Chorizo (page 110)

For the bean layer:

- 2 teaspoons mild vegetable oil
- 1 small red onion, half shredded, half finely diced (reserve for guacamole layer)
- ½ teaspoon ground cumin
- ¼ teaspoon onion powder
- ¼ teaspoon garlic powder
- 2 (15-ounce) cans pinto beans, drained and rinsed
- salt and freshly ground pepper to taste

For the guacamole layer:

- 4 large, ripe avocados
- 1 to 2 tablespoons lime juice
- 2 to 3 tablespoons fresh cilantro, chopped
- salt and freshly ground pepper to taste
- 1 (16-ounce) container sour cream
- 1 (24-ounce) jar chunky salsa (drain some of the liquid)
- 3 cups shredded cheddar cheese
- 3 to 4 green onions, just the green parts, chopped
- tortilla chips, to serve

1. In a skillet, heat the olive oil over medium heat, add the chorizo, and cook, stirring often, until slightly browned. Set aside to cool.

2. For the bean layer, in a large saucepan, heat the vegetable oil over medium heat. Add the shredded onion and cook until slightly soft, about 2 minutes. Add the cumin, onion powder, and garlic powder, and stir to combine. Add the pinto beans and cook until the beans are warm and softened, about 5 minutes. Remove from the heat and mash with a potato masher, adding a little water if needed, until chunky but creamy. Add salt and pepper to taste. Let cool.

3. For the guacamole, scoop out all of the avocado flesh into a large bowl. Add the finely diced onion (only use as much as you prefer), a little lime juice (increase as desired), cilantro, and salt and pepper to taste. Mash until well combined, adjusting the seasoning with more salt, pepper, and lime juice as desired.

4. In the bottom of a 9 x 13-inch pan, spread out the chorizo. Top with the cooled beans. Spread the guacamole over the beans. Add the sour cream on top of the guacamole, and then top the sour cream with the chunky salsa. Sprinkle the shredded cheese over the salsa and top with green onions.

5. Serve with tortilla chips and share with others, if you're feeling generous.

Southwest BBQ Chick'n Pizza

A little spice, a little tart, a lot of flavor. This is a favorite appetizer that comes together with a quickness.

Makes 4 to 5 servings

- 1 sheet puff pastry, defrosted but still chilled
- 1/4 cup Easy BBQ Sauce (page 55)
- 1/2 recipe Basic Chick'n (page 14), cut into thin, 2-inch-long strips
- 1 cup shredded mozzarella cheese
- 1/4 red onion, sliced into thin half moons
- 1/4 cup chopped cilantro

1. Preheat oven to 425°F and line a baking sheet with parchment paper. Unfold or unroll the puff pastry onto the parchment.
2. Spread the barbecue sauce across the puff pastry, leaving a 1/4-inch border around the edge.
3. Sprinkle Basic Chick'n evenly across the sauce, top with mozzarella, and sprinkle onion on top.
4. Bake for 15 to 20 minutes, until the cheese is golden and melted and the edges of the puff pastry are browned and puffy.
5. Remove from the oven and let cool slightly before sprinkling with cilantro and serving.

Ham, Cheese, and Asparagus Slab Pie

This slab pie is so fragrant, so elegant, and so delicious, you may not want to share it with anyone. No judgment.

Makes 4 to 5 servings

2 sheets puff pastry, defrosted but still chilled

2 tablespoons Dijon mustard

¼ teaspoon garlic powder

½ teaspoon dried oregano

½ recipe Basic Ham (page 18), thinly sliced

6 slices provolone or Swiss cheese

1 pound asparagus, rough ends trimmed, lightly steamed and blanched (thinner stalks are better)

2 tablespoons melted unsalted butter

1. Preheat the oven to 400°F. Line a baking sheet with parchment paper.
2. Unroll the puff pastry and gently fold each piece into a 10 x 10-inch square.
3. Place one piece of puff pastry on the baking sheet and spread with mustard, leaving a ½-inch border at the edges.
4. Sprinkle with the garlic powder and oregano.
5. Layer the ham in a single layer across the top of the mustard-covered puff pastry.
6. Add the cheese, keeping it within the ½-inch border.
7. Top with the steamed and blanched asparagus, spreading them out evenly.

8. Lightly brush the border of the puff pastry with a little melted butter.

9. Place the second square of puff pastry on top. Gently press the edges together, then fold the edges up and over, creating a double edge to the crust. Crimp the edges with a fork.

10. Brush the top with the remaining melted butter. Cut 2 or 3 small slits on top of the pastry, to vent and allow steam to escape.

11. Bake for 25 minutes, until puffed and golden brown. Let sit for 10 minutes before slicing into squares and serving.

Sausage-Stuffed Mushroom Caps

These mushroom caps are simple to make but complex in taste and presentation, making you effortlessly impressive. You can make the filling ahead of time so stuffing and baking the mushrooms is a cinch.

Makes 8 to 10 servings

- 20 large cremini mushrooms (1 inch or wider)
- 1 tablespoon olive oil
- 2 Italian Sausages (page 34), chopped into small chunks or roughly grated
- 2 cloves garlic, minced
- ¼ teaspoon onion powder
- 1 cup frozen spinach, thawed and drained
- salt and freshly ground pepper to taste
- ½ cup gorgonzola cheese
- 2 tablespoons crushed walnuts

1. Preheat the oven to 400°F. Line a rimmed baking sheet with parchment paper or foil. If using foil, spray a light coating of oil over it.
2. Carefully remove the stems from mushrooms. Scrape out any gills. Use a moist paper towel to clean any dirt off of the mushroom caps. Place each cap on the prepared baking sheet with the opening up and set aside.
3. In a large skillet, heat the oil over medium heat. Add the sausage and cook until it starts to brown, 3 to 5 minutes, stirring often. Add the garlic and onion powder and cook until fragrant, about 1 minute. Add the drained spinach and a little salt and pepper to taste. Stir to combine and remove from heat, then let cool slightly.

4. Stir in the gorgonzola and walnuts. Press spoonfuls of the mixture into the top of each prepared mushroom, filling them generously.

5. Spray or brush the filled mushrooms with a little olive oil and bake for 15 minutes or until the mixture is golden and the mushrooms are tender when pierced with a fork. Let cool slightly before serving.

Vegan variation: Omit the gorgonzola. Add 2 teaspoons mild miso and 1 tablespoon nutritional yeast right before the spinach is added, and stir to combine.

Homemade Pizza Rolls

Nothing says "after school snack" quite like pizza rolls. And even as a fully-fledged adult, I still get a hankering for them from time to time.

Makes about 25 rolls

½ cup warm water

½ teaspoon evaporated cane sugar

1 (.25-ounce) package rapid-rise yeast (2¼ teaspoons)

1½ cups unbleached all-purpose flour

¼ teaspoon salt

¼ cup unsalted butter, melted

½ recipe Sausage of the Summer (page 51), cut into tiny cubes

1½ cups shredded mozzarella

3 tablespoons dried oregano

olive oil

1 to 2 cups marinara or pizza sauce, for dipping

1. In a large bowl, combine the water and sugar, and stir. Add yeast and let sit until foamy, about 3 minutes.
2. In another bowl, combine the flour and salt. Add the butter to the yeast mixture and then add flour, ½ cup at a time, until a sticky dough forms.
3. Turn out onto a clean, floured surface and knead until smooth and elastic, about 5 minutes, adding flour as needed.
4. Place in an oiled bowl and turn to coat. Cover and let rise until doubled, about 1 hour.
5. Preheat the oven to 450°F. Set out the chopped seitan sausage, mozzarella, and oregano in individual bowls.

6. Roll out the dough into an 18 x 24-inch square and use a pizza cutter to cut it into strips about 1½ x 4 inches.

7. In the middle of one side of each strip, place a pinch each of seitan, mozzarella, and oregano. You need to be able to fold and seal them, so keep that in mind when filling. Distribute all of the filling components before sealing the strips, so you can see if you need to adjust your proportions.

8. Roll over the naked side of the strip to cover the filling and pinch to seal. You may need to brush with a little water to get the dough to seal.

9. Brush or spray with a light coating of olive oil.

10. Bake for 10 to 12 minutes, until lightly browned.

11. Serve warm with marinara sauce. The rolls reheat beautifully in a toaster oven.

Vegan variation: Replace the butter with non-dairy margarine. Replace the mozzarella with non-dairy cheese.

Macho Nachos

Nachos are a most versatile food: They can be an appetizer, they can be a stand-alone meal, they can be a close friend after a long day. Oh wait, maybe that's just me...

Makes 4 to 5 servings

- 8 ounces corn chips
- ½ recipe Ground Chorizo (page 110)
- 8 ounces cheddar cheese, shredded
- 3 cups shredded Pepper Jack cheese
- 1 (15-ounce) can black beans, rinsed and drained
- ¾ cup chopped red onions
- ½ cup black olives, sliced
- ½ cup cilantro, chopped
- guacamole, salsa, and sour cream, to serve

1. Preheat the oven to 400°F.
2. Spread half the corn chips in a single layer on a baking sheet. Top with half of the chorizo, half of the cheese, and half of the beans.
3. Repeat with the remaining chips, chorizo, cheese, and beans to make a second layer.
4. Bake for 10 minutes, or until the cheese is melted.
5. Top with red onions, black olives, and cilantro.
6. Serve immediately with guacamole, salsa, and sour cream.

Vegan variation: Replace the cheese with non-dairy shredded cheese.

Chick'n Fingers

Serve with Easy BBQ Sauce and Perfect Ranch Dipping Sauce.

Makes 4 to 5 servings

- 1 cup milk of choice
- 2 teaspoons garlic powder, divided
- 2 teaspoons paprika, divided
- sprinkle of salt and freshly ground pepper
- 1 ½ cups plus 2 tablespoons unbleached all-purpose flour, divided
- 1 teaspoon baking powder
- 1 recipe Chick'n Wings (page 29), cut in half lengthwise
- 3 to 4 cups mild vegetable oil, for frying
- Easy BBQ Sauce (page 55) and Perfect Ranch Dipping Sauce (page 57), to serve

1. In a shallow bowl, combine the milk, 1 teaspoon of the garlic powder, 1 teaspoon of the paprika, a sprinkle of salt and pepper, and 2 tablespoons of the flour, and whisk to create a slurry.
2. In a separate bowl, whisk together the remaining flour, garlic powder, paprika, baking powder, and another crack of pepper.
3. Dip each Chick'n Wing into the wet mixture and coat. Dredge through the dry mix to coat and set aside on a piece of waxed paper on a clean plate.
4. Fill a wide pan with high sides ½ inch deep with oil. Heat over medium-high until a little splash of batter sizzles and browns.
5. Gently add Chick'n Wings, a handful per batch, and cook until golden, flipping once, about 2 to 3 minutes per

side. Remove from the pan and place on a plate lined with paper towels. Repeat with the remaining Chick'n.

6. Serve warm with dipping sauces.

Soups and Stews

From thick and hearty to light and vibrant, the veggie-filled recipes within will nourish and comfort while providing a full meal, complete with veggies and protein. Serve with a salad and one of the accompanying bread recipes, and know that life is good.

Italian Wedding Soup

What a perfect way to showcase tasty meatballs! If you're planning ahead to make this soup, make the meatballs smaller, about half as big as indicated, so they'll nicely sit on a soup spoon when scooped up. Although, no one ever complained about a hefty meatball.

Makes 4 to 5 generous servings

- 3 tablespoons olive oil, divided
- 3 cloves garlic, minced
- 5 cups low-sodium vegetable broth
- ⅔ cup Israeli couscous
- 2 cups baby spinach, roughly chopped
- ½ cup grated carrot
- 3 tablespoons Italian parsley, chopped
- salt and freshly ground pepper to taste
- ½ recipe Meaty-Spheres (page 47)
- grated Parmesan cheese (optional)

1. In a large stock pot, heat 2 tablespoons of the oil over medium heat. Add the garlic and cook until fragrant, 2 minutes.
2. Add the vegetable broth and the couscous and cook until tender, 10 to 15 minutes.
3. Add the spinach, carrot, and parsley and cook until spinach is wilted. Season with salt and pepper to taste.
4. In a large skillet, heat the remaining 1 tablespoon of oil. Cook the meatballs until slightly golden, about 5 minutes. Add to the soup.
5. Garnish the soup with Parmesan to serve.

Ultimate Veggie Chili

This chili recipe always receives rave reviews. It's thick, hearty, and flavorful, providing healthy comfort that you can feel good about...even when dipping in for seconds. Serve it with a side salad and the Ultimate Cornbread (page 181) and call it a meal.

Makes 5 to 6 generous servings

- 2 tablespoons olive oil
- 1 medium yellow onion, diced
- 3 cloves garlic, minced
- 3 tablespoons chili powder
- 1 tablespoon ground cumin
- 2 teaspoons unsweetened cocoa powder
- 2 teaspoons ground coriander
- 1 teaspoon paprika
- ¼ to ½ teaspoon salt, as desired
- ¼ to ½ teaspoon cayenne pepper, as desired
- ¼ teaspoon ground cinnamon
- 1 recipe Ground Not-Beef (page 26)
- 1 bell pepper (your choice of color), seeded and diced
- 2 medium sweet potatoes, peeled and cut into ½-inch dice
- 1 (15-ounce) can tomato sauce
- 1 (28-ounce) can crushed tomatoes
- 1 (15-ounce) can pinto beans, rinsed and drained
- 1 (15-ounce) can kidney beans, rinsed and drained
- 1 (15-ounce) can black beans, rinsed and drained
- ½ to 1 cup water
- 2 zucchinis, sliced into ½-inch half moons
- 1 cup sweet corn, fresh or frozen, thawed
- freshly ground pepper to taste
- toppings of your choice: shredded cheese, sour cream, green onions, avocado, etc.

1. In a large stock pot, heat the oil over medium heat. Sauté the onion for 3 to 4 minutes, then add the garlic and cook, stirring often, until fragrant, about a minute.
2. Add the chili powder, cumin, cocoa, coriander, paprika, salt, cayenne, and cinnamon, and stir to coat the onions with the spices.
3. Stirring often and adding a splash of water if needed, let the spices open and become fragrant, about a minute.
4. Add the Ground Not-Beef and mix to combine, again adding a splash of water as needed, until it's a little browned.
5. Add the bell pepper and sweet potatoes. Again add a little splash of water to keep things from sticking, and lower the heat to medium-low. Cover and cook for 3 to 5 minutes, until the bell pepper is slightly softened.
6. Add the tomato sauce, crushed tomatoes, pinto beans, kidney beans, and black beans, and stir to combine. Increase the heat and let it come to a boil, stirring often. Lower it to a simmer and cook, stirring often, for at least an hour, until the sweet potatoes are tender and the chili is very fragrant.
7. Taste and adjust the seasoning with salt and pepper as needed. Add water, ¼ cup at a time, as needed, to keep it thick and saucy.
8. A half-hour before serving, add the zucchini and stir to combine. Once the zucchini is cooked through, add the corn, stir, and turn off the heat. Let the chili sit for 5 minutes before serving with toppings of your choice.

Note: Like many spiced things, this chili's flavor intensifies with time, so the longer you can simmer it, the tastier it will be. Just remember to stir it and add water as needed.

No-Beef Tip Stew

This recipe demands to be made in the depths of winter, when the only things you want are cushy blankets, Netflix, and comfort food. Serve with a side of greens and thick, crusty bread to sop up the juices.

Makes 5 to 6 generous servings

1 recipe No-Beef Tips (page 31)

2 tablespoons olive oil

1 medium yellow onion, diced

4 large carrots, peeled and cut into ½-inch-thick pieces

2 stalks celery, chopped into ¼-inch pieces

4 cloves garlic, chopped

1 teaspoon dried thyme

1 pound red or Yukon Gold potatoes, unpeeled, cut into 1-inch cubes

2 tablespoons unbleached all-purpose flour

1 ½ cups good-quality red wine

1 pound cremini mushrooms, quartered

3 to 4 cups low-sodium vegetable broth or beefless stock

2 bay leaves

salt and freshly ground pepper to taste

1. Make sure the No-Beef Tips are seared per the directions in that recipe. This will help the seitan retain a meaty texture in the stew.

2. In a large stock pot, heat the oil over medium heat. Add the onion and cook until slightly translucent, 3 to 5 minutes. Add the carrots and celery and cook, stirring often, until the carrots become vibrant in color, about 3 minutes. Add the garlic and thyme and cook until fragrant, another minute, before adding the potatoes.

3. In a medium bowl, whisk together the flour and red wine, working out the clumps.
4. Add the wine mixture to the pot and bring to a boil. Scrape the bottom to deglaze the pot.
5. Add the sliced mushrooms and lower to a simmer.
6. Add the vegetable broth, starting with just 2 cups, and the bay leaves. Cook, covered, stirring often, until the potatoes are still firm but starting to soften, about 30 minutes. Add more vegetable broth as needed if it's getting too thick. Add salt and pepper to taste.
7. Add the No-Beef Tips and continue cooking until potatoes are tender, about 15 minutes. Remove the bay leaves before serving.

Smoky Split Pea Soup

We eat this soup in our house a lot in the winter. It's a reliable standby that's hearty without being too rich or labor-intensive for a work night. Sop up the thick, green ambrosia with Soda Drop Biscuits (page 184) or a hearty bread of your choosing.

Makes 4 to 5 generous servings

- 3 tablespoons olive oil, divided
- 6 slices of Seitan Fakin' Bacon (page 42), chopped
- 1 to 2 tablespoons water
- ½ teaspoon liquid smoke (optional)
- 1 small yellow onion, chopped
- 2 cloves garlic, minced
- ½ teaspoons dried thyme
- 2 stalks celery, chopped into ½-inch pieces
- 3 carrots, peeled and chopped into ½-inch chunks
- 1 large red or yellow potato, diced to ½-inch chunks
- 2 cups dried split green peas, sorted and rinsed
- 7 to 8 cups low-sodium vegetable broth
- 1 bay leaf
- salt and freshly ground pepper to taste

1. In a large skillet, heat 1 tablespoon of the olive oil. Add the Fakin' and cook until warmed through, stirring often, about 3 to 5 minutes.
2. Add the water. Sprinkle with liquid smoke, if you want it smokier, and stir to combine well.
3. Cook until browned, about 3 to 5 minutes, adding a splash of water as needed to keep the seitan from sticking. Remove from the heat and set aside.

4. In a large stock pot, heat the remaining 2 tablespoons of olive oil. Add the onion and cook until translucent, about 5 minutes.
5. Add the garlic and thyme and cook until fragrant, about 2 minutes, stirring often.
6. Add the celery, carrots, and potatoes and stir to coat. Add a little salt and a crack of pepper.
7. Add the split peas, 7 cups of the vegetable broth, and the bay leaf.
8. Bring to a boil, then lower to a simmer and cook, covered, stirring often, until the split peas are very tender, about 45 minutes. Add more broth as needed, but keep the consistency thick.
9. Roughly blend soup with an immersion blender or carefully puree three-quarters of it in a blender or food processor. Add salt and pepper to taste.
10. Serve the hot soup with chunks of smoky seitan on top.

Meaty Mushroom Soup

This soup is thick and creamy, has a nuanced flavor, and is packed with nutty rice and chewy seitan, making it a very flavorful and satisfying meal.

Makes 4 to 5 generous servings

- 3 tablespoons olive oil, divided
- 1 medium onion, chopped
- 1 tablespoon soy sauce
- 3 cloves garlic, minced
- 2 carrots, peeled and chopped into ½-inch dice
- 2 stalks celery, chopped into ½-inch dice
- 1 teaspoon dried rosemary
- ½ teaspoon dried thyme
- 4 to 5 cups chopped mushrooms (a combination of cremini and portobello are fantastic)
- 4 cups low-sodium vegetable broth
- 1 cup uncooked brown or wild rice
- ½ recipe Chick'n Wings (page 29)
- salt and freshly ground pepper to taste

1. In a stock pot, heat 2 tablespoons of the oil over medium heat.
2. Add the onion and cook until it begins to soften and become fragrant, about 3 to 5 minutes. Add the soy sauce and garlic and cook until fragrant.
3. Add the carrots, celery, rosemary, and thyme, and stir to combine.
4. And the mushrooms and cook until they begin to soften and release their juices, about 5 to 8 minutes, stirring often.

5. Add the vegetable broth and rice. Bring to a boil. Lower and cover, simmering and stirring often, until the rice is cooked through, about 35 to 45 minutes.

6. Using an immersion blender or a regular blender or food processor, process one-half of the soup until creamy. Return to the pot and stir to combine. Adjust to taste with salt and pepper.

7. In a skillet, heat the remaining 1 tablespoon of olive oil over medium heat. Sauté the Chick'n Wings until golden, about 5 minutes, and add to the soup before serving.

Best Veggie Matzo Ball Soup Evah

We take matzo ball soup seriously in our house. Many people do. But we've mastered the elusive vegetarian version, which many people refuse to believe exists. Whether you're celebrating a holiday or are sick and need a shot of Jewish penicillin, this recipe has you covered—chicken-free. Take note, though, that this rich, flavorful veggie stock might be a little darker colored than you're used to. That color is all flavor. If you've never made matzo ball soup before, note that you'll need 2 large stock pots—one for the broth and one for the matzo balls.

Makes 4 servings

For the matzo balls:

- ½ cup matzo meal
- ¼ teaspoon baking powder
- ⅛ teaspoon grated nutmeg
- sprinkle of salt and freshly ground pepper
- 2 large eggs
- 2 tablespoons mild vegetable oil
- 10 cups water
- ¼ cup soy sauce

For the veggie stock:

- 3 tablespoons olive oil
- 1 large onion, quartered
- 8 cloves garlic, crushed
- 1 large leek, rough greens and end removed, roughly chopped
- 6 large carrots, divided
- 4 stalks celery, roughly chopped
- 1 parsnip, end removed and roughly chopped
- 8 cups water
- ½ recipe Chick'n Wings (page 29), cut into long slices
- salt and freshly ground pepper to taste
- Fresh dill for garnish

1. For the matzo balls, in a medium bowl, combine the matzo meal, baking powder, nutmeg, salt, and pepper. In a small bowl, whisk the eggs. Add the vegetable oil to the eggs and whisk to combine. Add the wet ingredients to the dry and whisk to combine. Cover and refrigerate for at least an hour before using. Prepare a stock pot with the 10 cups of water and soy sauce.

2. For the veggie stock, in a separate stock pot, heat 2 tablespoons of olive oil over medium low heat. Add the onion and cook until all sides are browned, stirring often. Add a splash of water as needed to keep from sticking and to deglaze the pan. Continue cooking, making sure the onions don't burn, but turn very brown. Add the garlic and chopped leek and cook until they are golden, adding a splash of water as needed. Trim the ends and roughly chop 3 of the carrots, and add to the broth along with the celery and parsnip and stir to combine. Cover with the 8 cups of water, a crack of pepper, and a sprinkle of salt. Bring to a boil then lower the temp to a simmer. Cover and let cook until the veggies are very cooked down, about 40 minutes. Taste and add salt and pepper as needed. Strain the veggies and discard, leaving just the broth. Turn off the heat.

3. Once the broth is resting, bring the water with the soy sauce to a boil. Remove the matzo ball mix from the fridge and use a cookie scoop to scoop out balls about 2 tablespoons in size. They will look small, but keep in mind they will expand 3 to 4 times this size when cooked. Roll between your hands to round the edges and gently compress the mixture. Prepare all of the matzo balls before cooking, placing the prepped balls on a sheet of waxed paper.

4. Using a slotted spoon, gently add the matzo balls to the boiling water. Cover with a lid, reduce the heat to a simmer, and cook for 20 minutes without removing the lid.

5. While the matzo balls are cooking, peel the remaining 3 carrots and cut into ¼-inch coins. Add the carrot coins to the broth and bring back up to a simmer. Cook until the carrots are tender but still firm, about 10 minutes.

6. In a skillet, heat the remaining tablespoon of olive oil over medium heat. Add the chick'n and cook until slightly golden, about 5 minutes. Remove from the heat and set aside.

7. To serve, ladle broth into bowls, including a couple of carrot coins. Add a couple chunks of Chick'n. Top with 2 to 3 matzo balls and a sprig of fresh dill.

Vegan variation: I'll be honest—the vegan matzo balls will not please purists as they are really dense and more dumpling-like. That said, they are tasty in their own right. Replace the eggs in the matzo batter with ½ cup silken tofu that has been pureed until smooth.

Curried Seitan Stew

This recipe is tasty served with a variety of sides—try potatoes, plain rice, or Fragrant Rice (page 186). Any way you pair it, this stew is a surefire winner. The mango adds bursts of sweetness and a complex flavor that makes this stew intoxicatingly delicious.

Makes 4 servings

- 3 tablespoons unbleached all-purpose flour
- 1 tablespoon curry powder
- 2 teaspoons garam masala
- ¼ teaspoon salt
- 1 recipe Basic Chick'n (page 14), cut into 1-inch chunks
- 2 tablespoons mild vegetable oil
- 1 red onion, sliced
- 1 slightly under-ripe mango, peeled and cubed
- 2 tablespoons brown sugar
- 1 (14-ounce) can light coconut milk

1. Mix the flour, curry powder, garam masala, and salt in a large plastic bag or brown paper lunch bag. Add the seitan and shake to coat. Save any extra seasoning mix that doesn't stick.

2. In a large skillet, heat the oil over medium heat. Add the seitan and cook until browned, about 5 minutes, stirring often.

3. Reduce the heat to low. Add the onion and mango, and cook, stirring, for 2 to 3 minutes.

4. Stir in the brown sugar, any remaining seasoning, and coconut milk.

5. Simmer, covered, for about 10 minutes, until the sauce is thick and fragrant, the onion is slightly cooked down, and the mango is tender.

Phast Pho

Whether you want a fresh, fragrant bowl of soup or are tending to a hangover, pho has you covered. Enjoy this with some tasty seitan Basic Beef slices and it will stick to your ribs.

Makes 4 servings

For the broth:

- 2 tablespoons mild vegetable oil
- 2 large yellow onions, quartered
- 1 (4-inch) piece fresh ginger, peeled and quartered
- 2 whole cinnamon sticks
- 2 whole star anise
- 1 teaspoon whole coriander seeds
- 6 cups low-sodium beefless broth (or use beef-free bouillon dissolved in water)
- 2 tablespoons soy sauce
- 8 ounces dried rice noodles
- 1 tablespoon mild vegetable oil
- ½ recipe Basic Beef (page 16), cut into long, thin slices
- 2 limes
- 4 green onions
- 1 jalapeño pepper
- 1 ½ cups fresh basil or Thai basil
- 2 cups bean sprouts
- 3 carrots, cut into thin matchsticks
- sriracha or other hot sauce, to serve

1. For the broth, in a large stock pot, heat the vegetable oil.
2. Add the onions and ginger and cook, stirring often, until golden and very fragrant, about 5 minutes. Remove the pot from the heat and set aside.

3. In a dry skillet, add the cinnamon sticks and star anise. Over medium heat, cook, stirring often, to toast the spices. Once fragrant, add the coriander and continue to stir often, lowering the heat if needed to avoid burning, until very fragrant, 2 more minutes. The coriander might pop.

4. Add the toasted spices to the onion and ginger and cover with broth and soy sauce. Return to the heat, bring to a boil, then lower to a simmer and cook for about 25 minutes, allowing the flavor to permeate the broth.

5. Prepare the rice noodles according to the package directions. Once drained, they will start to stick together, so rinse with cool water and toss with a tiny amount of mild vegetable oil. Set aside.

6. In a skillet, heat the 1 tablespoon oil and cook the slices of beef until browned, about 5 minutes. Set side.

7. Prepare the garnishes in separate bowls. Quarter the limes, chop the green onions, slice the jalapeño pepper, remove the basil leaves from the stems, and rinse the sprouts.

8. Pour the broth through a fine-mesh sieve to remove the solids. Bring the broth back up to a high simmer.

9. To serve, place a scoop of noodles in the bottom of a bowl. Add some carrots sticks. Cover with broth and top with some crisped beef. Top with garnishes and hot sauce as desired.

Seitan Masala

Fragrant and complexly flavored, masala is a perennial Indian favorite. Ditch the chickpeas and enjoy it with your handy-dandy seitan. Serve over the Fragrant Rice or plain basmati, or with naan.

Makes 4 servings

- ½ cup plain yogurt (not Greek)
- 3 teaspoons garam masala, divided
- 1 teaspoon ground coriander
- ¼ teaspoon salt
- 1 recipe Basic Chick'n (page 14) or Basic Beef (page 16), cut into chunks
- 2 tablespoons mild vegetable oil
- 1 large onion, cut into thin half moons
- 1 tablespoon grated fresh ginger
- 3 cloves garlic, grated
- 2 teaspoons ground cumin
- 1 teaspoon ground turmeric
- ½ teaspoon ground cinnamon
- ¼ to ½ teaspoon cayenne pepper, as desired
- 1 tablespoon tomato paste
- 1 (15-ounce) can crushed tomatoes
- ½ cup milk of choice
- cooked plain rice, Fragrant Rice (page 186), or naan, to serve
- chopped fresh cilantro, to serve

1. In a large bowl, combine the yogurt, 2 teaspoons of the garam masala, and the coriander and salt.
2. Add the seitan and mix to combine. Cover and refrigerate for 1 hour.
3. In a large skillet, heat the vegetable oil over medium heat. Add the onion and cook until softened, about 5

minutes. Add the ginger, garlic, remaining 1 teaspoon garam masala, cumin, turmeric, cinnamon, and cayenne. Stir the spices to coat the onion and cook until fragrant, about a minute.

4. Add the tomato paste and stir to combine.
5. Using a slotted spoon, remove the seitan from the yogurt mixture and add to the skillet. Cover with the crushed tomatoes and stir to combine. Gently whisk in the milk.
6. Simmer, uncovered, over low heat until the sauce thickens, about 15 minutes. Add salt as needed.
7. Serve with plain rice, Fragrant Rice, or naan. Garnish with chopped fresh cilantro.

Vegan variation: Replace the yogurt and milk with non-dairy versions.

Mighty, Meaty Minestrone

Brothy, vegetable-packed soup meets Italian sausages. It's a natural pairing. Sop up the broth with Buttery Biscuits (see page 182) and call it a meal.

Makes 4 servings

- 1 tablespoon plus 2 teaspoons olive oil, divided
- 1 small yellow onion, chopped
- 3 cloves garlic, minced
- 2 teaspoons dried oregano
- 1 teaspoon dried thyme
- 2 medium carrots, chopped to ½-inch chunks
- 2 stalks celery, chopped to ½-inch chunks
- 6 cups low-sodium vegetable broth
- 1 (15-ounce) can navy or cannellini beans, drained and rinsed
- 1 cup dried barley, rinsed
- 1 (15-ounce) can crushed tomatoes with juice
- 2 cups chopped greens (kale, spinach)
- 3 Italian Sausages (page 34), cut into ½-inch coins
- salt and freshly ground pepper to taste

1. In a large stock pot, heat 1 tablespoon of the olive oil over medium heat and sauté the onion for about 2 minutes.
2. Add the garlic and continue cooking until the onion is translucent, about 3 to 5 more minutes.
3. Add the oregano and thyme and cook, stirring, for about a minute, or until fragrant.
4. Incorporate the carrots and celery and sauté for about 5 minutes, stirring often, until vibrant in color.

5. Add the vegetable broth and increase the heat to medium-high, bringing to a boil.
6. Add the beans and barley and lower the heat to medium. Let the soup simmer, covered, until the barley is tender, about 40 minutes.
7. Add the canned tomatoes, with their juice, and cook until heated through, about 10 minutes.
8. Remove the soup from heat and add the chopped greens. Stir to combine and wilt the greens. Season with salt and pepper to taste.
9. In a skillet, heat the remaining 2 teaspoons of oil and cook the sausages until golden, about 5 minutes.
10. Serve the soup with sausage pieces on top.

Gimme Some Goulash

Goulash, the homemade predecessor to Hamburger Helper. Think what you will of the anthropomorphized glove, this recipe has earned its rightful place in the American canon of classic comfort meals. Plus, you can make it one pot, and that always earns a recipe extra points.

Makes 4 to 5 generous servings

- 2 tablespoons mild vegetable oil
- 2 large yellow onions, chopped
- 2 red bell peppers, seeded and chopped
- 1 recipe Ground Not-Beef (page 26)
- 3 cloves garlic, minced
- 3 tablespoons paprika, preferably sweet
- 1 teaspoon caraway seeds
- 1/4 cup unbleached all-purpose flour
- 1/4 cup red wine vinegar
- 1/4 cup tomato paste
- 1 (15-ounce) can diced tomatoes
- 4 to 5 cups low-sodium vegetable broth
- 1 1/2 cups dried elbow macaroni
- salt and freshly ground pepper to taste

1. In a large stock pot, heat the oil over medium heat. Add the onions and bell pepper, and cook until the onions are translucent, about 5 minutes.
2. Add the Ground Not-Beef and garlic and cook until fragrant, about another minute.
3. Add the paprika, caraway seeds, and flour, and cook until combined and the onions are well coated.
4. Whisk in the vinegar and tomato paste.

5. Gently mix in the tomatoes, with their juices, and add 2 cups of broth.
6. Bring mixture to a boil, stirring often. Once it reaches a boil, add the elbow macaroni and stir to combine.
7. Add 2 more cups of vegetable broth and bring the mixture back to a boil.
8. Lower to a simmer, cover, and let cook until the macaroni is tender, about 20 minutes. Stir often and add extra vegetable broth if it starts to get too thick.
9. Season to taste with salt and pepper.

Corn Chowder

Spicy sausage bites between spoonfuls of creamy sweet corn make this a refreshing and flavorful summer soup. Serve with a side salad and some crusty bread.

Makes 4 to 5 servings

- 3 tablespoons unsalted butter
- 1 medium yellow onion, chopped
- 2 cloves garlic, minced
- 1 teaspoon dried thyme
- 5 cups low-sodium vegetable broth
- 3 large Yukon gold potatoes, peeled and cut into ½-inch cubes
- 1 bay leaf
- salt and freshly ground pepper to taste
- 8 ears fresh sweet yellow corn kernels, cut from the cob
- ½ cup milk of choice
- 2 teaspoons olive oil
- ½ recipe Italian Sausages (page 34), cut into ½-inch coins
- 2 to 3 tablespoons chopped fresh chives, to serve

1. Melt the butter in a stock pot over medium heat. Add the onion and cook until translucent, about 5 to 7 minutes.
2. Add the garlic and thyme and cook until fragrant, about 1 minute.
3. Add the vegetable broth and bring to a boil, stirring constantly, then add the potatoes.
4. Add the bay leaf and season with salt and pepper to taste. Bring back up to a boil, then reduce the heat to medium-low and allow to simmer, stirring occasionally, until the potatoes are tender, about 20 minutes.

5. Add the corn and cook until heated through, about 2 minutes.
6. Remove the bay leaf and transfer 2½ cups of the chowder to a blender. Puree until smooth. Stir the mixture back into the pot, then stir in the milk.
7. In a skillet, heat the olive oil and cook the sausages until golden, about 5 minutes.
8. Serve the soup with sausage pieces on top. Sprinkle each serving with chives.

Tortilla Soup

This soup is delicious, flavorful, and smells like heaven. Add some jalapeño or serrano pepper if you like to spice things up a little.

Makes 4 servings

- 2 tablespoons mild vegetable oil, divided
- 1 medium yellow onion, chopped
- 3 cloves garlic, minced
- 2 teaspoons chili powder
- 1 teaspoon ground cumin
- 1 teaspoon paprika
- 4 cups low-sodium vegetable broth
- 1 (14-ounce) can diced tomatoes
- 1 (4-ounce) can diced tomatoes with green chilies
- ¼ cup masa harina
- 1 cup milk of choice
- 1 (15-ounce) can black beans, drained and rinsed
- 1 (15-ounce) can pinto beans, drained and rinsed
- 1 cup corn, fresh or frozen
- ½ cup sour cream
- salt and freshly ground pepper to taste
- 1 recipe Chick'n Wings (page 29), cut into strips
- shredded cheese, tortilla chips, salsa, avocado, fresh cilantro, lime wedges, for serving

1. Heat 1 tablespoon of the oil in a large stock pot over medium heat. Cook the onion for 5 to 7 minutes until translucent.
2. Add the garlic, chili powder, cumin, and paprika, and cook until fragrant, about 2 minutes.
3. Add the vegetable broth, diced tomatoes, and tomatoes with green chilies, and bring to a boil.

4. Add the masa harina and whisk to incorporate, bringing the mixture back up to a boil. Lower to a simmer and slowly incorporate the milk, black beans, and pinto beans.
5. Simmer, covered, until heated through, about 10 minutes. Mix in the corn and sour cream. Whisk to incorporate, and add salt and pepper to taste. Cook until fully heated through.
6. In a separate pan, heat the remaining oil and add the seitan. Cook until browned, stirring often, about 10 minutes. Add to the soup and mix to combine.
7. Serve with an assortment of garnishes as desired.

Vegan variation: Use non-dairy sour cream.

Lunch and Lighter Fare

Whether you need a light meal, lunch, or a quick nosh, this chapter has you covered. Take your seitan making to the next level with these tasty meals that will fuel you while also pleasing your taste buds.

Avocado Not-Chicken Salad Sandwiches

This recipe is creamy, sweet, and filling, while feeling fresh. Perfect for summer lunches or picnics. Serve with Happy Piggy Succotash (page 185) for a perfect summer meal.

Makes 4 sandwiches

- 2 teaspoons mild vegetable oil
- ½ recipe Basic Chick'n (page 14), cut into small ½-inch dice
- 2 large ripe avocados
- ¼ cup of mayonnaise
- 2 teaspoons lime juice
- 1 sweet apple (like Gala), peeled and chopped
- ¼ cup diced celery
- ¼ cup diced red onion
- 2 tablespoons cilantro, chopped
- ¼ teaspoon salt
- freshly ground pepper to taste
- 8 slices of hearty but soft sandwich bread

1. Heat the oil in a skillet. Add the seitan and cook until lightly golden, stirring often, about 5 minutes. Remove from the heat and let cool completely.
2. In a large bowl, mash the avocados.
3. Add the mayo and stir until creamy.
4. Stir in the lime juice, then add the seitan, apple, celery, and red onion, and stir to coat.
5. Add the cilantro, salt, and pepper to taste.
6. Spread the salad on bread to serve.

Vegan variation: Use vegan mayonnaise.

Pulled Pork-ish Sandwiches with Creamy Slaw

This recipe is summer in a bun. Tangy barbecue-smothered seitan topped with creamy, crunchy slaw, both of which can be made well ahead of time and brought out at any moment to delight your guests. The pulled pork-ish can be made in a slow cooker and kept warm on low.

Makes 4 to 6 sandwiches

1 recipe Basic Seitan 2.0 (page 12)

1 to 2 tablespoons olive oil

2 tablespoons soy sauce

1 teaspoon honey or agave

freshly ground pepper to taste

1 recipe Easy BBQ Sauce (page 55)

1 package buns

1 recipe Creamy Slaw (recipe follows)

1. Shred the seitan into long shreds using a vegetable peeler, or cut into long, narrow slivers.
2. Heat the oil in a large pan. Add the soy sauce and honey or agave, and whisk to combine. Add the seitan and mix to combine. Sprinkle with pepper and cook until slightly browned.
3. If cooking on the stovetop, add enough barbecue sauce to thoroughly coat the seitan. Let simmer on low for at least an hour, so the flavors can meld. If cooking in a slow cooker spray or wipe the slow cooker dish with oil and transfer the seitan mixture to the pot. Heat on low, stirring occasionally, until ready to serve. Add more sauce as needed.
4. Serve on buns, with a scoop of slaw on top of the seitan.

Creamy Slaw

Crunchy, creamy, with a little zip. This is lighter than the slaw you grew up eating, but still comforting.

Makes 5 to 6 cups

1 pound shredded cabbage (red, green, or a mixture), about 1 small head

1 tablespoon salt

1 large carrot, shredded into large strands

⅓ cup mayonnaise

⅓ cup sour cream

2 tablespoons evaporated cane sugar

2 tablespoons apple cider vinegar

1 teaspoon Dijon mustard

½ teaspoon celery salt

freshly ground pepper to taste

1. Toss the cabbage with the salt and place in a colander, over the sink, for 5 minutes to let the cabbage drain its water. Lightly rinse with cold water and lightly dry with a paper towel. Add the shredded carrots. Set aside in a large bowl.
2. In a small bowl, whisk together the mayonnaise, sour cream, sugar, apple cider vinegar, mustard, celery salt, and a sprinkle of pepper.
3. Add the mayonnaise mixture to the cabbage in batches, tossing to mix as you go, until it's just coated. Taste to determine if you want more dressing.
4. Serve with Pulled Pork-ish Sandwiches (above) or as a summer side dish.

Vegan variation: Use vegan mayonnaise and sour cream.

Taco Tuesday

Taco Tuesday is observed weekly in our house...just not always on Tuesday. Tacos are great because they come together quickly and can utilize a variety of toppings, keeping things fresh and interesting. Here, we explore a basic recipe. Alternatively, try out Ground Chorizo (page 110) for a different spin on the classic.

Makes 10 to 12 tacos

1 tablespoon chili powder

1 ½ teaspoons ground cumin

½ teaspoon onion powder

½ teaspoon garlic powder

½ teaspoon paprika

½ teaspoon dried oregano

¼ teaspoon cayenne pepper, or as desired

¼ teaspoon salt

sprinkle of freshly ground pepper to taste

2 tablespoons mild vegetable oil, plus more as needed

½ yellow onion, finely chopped

1 recipe Ground Not-Beef (page 26)

1 large bell pepper (color of your choice), seeded and cut into a small dice

1 cup sweet corn (fresh or frozen)

warm tortillas, shredded cheese, salsa, guacamole, sour cream, and lettuce, to serve

1. In a small bowl, combine the chili powder, cumin, onion powder, garlic powder, paprika, oregano, cayenne, salt, and black pepper.

2. Heat the oil in the bottom of a large skillet over medium heat, and sauté the onion until slightly translucent, about 2 minutes. Add the spice blend and cook until fragrant, about a minute.

3. Add the Ground Not-Beef and stir to combine. Add a splash of water as needed to keep it from burning.
4. In a separate skillet, add a little oil and the bell pepper. Cook for about 1 minute, on medium heat, before reducing the heat to medium-low.
5. Add the corn and a sprinkle of salt and pepper. Cook until the bell pepper is slightly softened and the corn is warmed through, but crisp.
6. Serve the taco meat and bell pepper mixtures with warmed tortillas and other fixings.

Ground Chorizo

Add some spice to your life with tasty, zesty chorizo! Top your tacos, stuff your burritos, stir into your eggs—it's a flavor explosion. If you can't find ancho chili powder, use 1 tablespoon regular chili powder with 1 teaspoon paprika.

Makes 2½ cups

- 2 tablespoons olive oil
- 1 small yellow onion, chopped
- 2 cloves garlic, minced
- 1 tablespoon plus 1 teaspoon ancho chili powder
- 1 teaspoon ground cumin
- ½ teaspoon ground coriander
- ½ teaspoon dried oregano
- ⅛ teaspoon ground cinnamon
- ⅛ teaspoon salt
- freshly ground pepper to taste
- 1 recipe Ground Not-Beef (page 26)

1. In a large skillet, heat the olive oil over medium-low heat. Sauté the onion until translucent. Add the garlic and sauté until fragrant, about a minute.
2. Add the chili powder, cumin, coriander, oregano, cinnamon, salt, and pepper, and stir to combine. Increase the heat to medium, add the Ground Not-Beef, and stir to combine, adding a splash of water as needed to deglaze the pan and help incorporate the seasoning into the seitan.
3. Cook until the seitan is lightly browned. Remove from the heat and use as desired.

Steak Salad

This salad is hearty and filling, with a tasty tang from the dressing.

Makes 2 to 3 large servings or 4 to 5 sides

1 tablespoon mild vegetable oil

2 tablespoons soy sauce

½ teaspoon garlic powder

½ recipe Ribs (page 31), not seared, sliced thin

2 to 3 tablespoons balsamic vinegar

3 tablespoons olive oil

1 to 2 teaspoons Dijon mustard, as desired

1 clove garlic, crushed

6 cups mixed salad greens

1 avocado, cubed

¼ red onion, thinly sliced

⅔ cup cherry tomatoes, sliced

4 ounces crumbled blue cheese

salt and freshly ground pepper to taste

1. In a small bowl, whisk together the vegetable oil, soy sauce, garlic powder, and a couple cracks of fresh pepper.
2. Heat a skillet over medium heat and add the soy sauce mixture. Lay the ribs in the skillet in an even layer and cook until browned, stirring often. Once cooked, set aside to cool slightly.
3. In a small bowl, whisk together the vinegar, olive oil, mustard, garlic, and salt and pepper to taste.
4. To serve, place greens in a large salad bowl. Toss with enough of the dressing to lightly coat.
5. Top with avocado, red onion, tomatoes, blue cheese, and seitan. Drizzle with any remaining dressing. Serve immediately.

Bahn Mi

If you've never had bahn mi, you're in for a treat. Fresh, fragrant, and tangy, it's truly a delightful sandwich for the senses. The pickled veggies taste best if made a day or two ahead of time. But if you're really hankering for a sammie, a couple of hours of chill time will suffice.

Makes 4 to 5 sandwiches

- 1 to 2 teaspoons mild vegetable oil
- 3 cloves garlic, grated or minced
- 2 tablespoons soy sauce
- 1 tablespoon evaporated cane sugar
- ½ teaspoon ground lemongrass
- ½ teaspoon ground coriander
- ½ recipe Basic Chick'n (page 14), cut into thin slices
- ½ cup mayonnaise
- 1 teaspoon lime juice
- ½ teaspoon lime zest
- 1 to 2 teaspoons sriracha (optional)
- 4 to 5 Vietnamese or French baguettes
- 1 recipe Pickled Vegetables (page 180)
- sliced jalapeños (optional)
- fresh cilantro leaves

1. In a large skillet, heat the oil over medium heat. Add the garlic and cook until fragrant, 1 minute.
2. Add the soy sauce and reduce the heat to medium-low.
3. In a small bowl, combine the sugar, lemongrass, and coriander, and sprinkle over the soy sauce.
4. Add the seitan in a thin layer and cook until edges brown a little, about 5 minutes, flipping halfway through.

5. In a small bowl, whisk together the mayonnaise, lime juice and zest, and sriracha, if using.

6. Cut baguettes in half and spread with a smear of the mayo mixture.

7. Add a few seitan slices, pickled veggies, jalapeños, if using, and cilantro.

Vegan variation: Use vegan mayonnaise.

Ultimate Not-Steak Fajitas

Tangy, fragrant, and fillable—fajitas are the perfect food for a quick weeknight dinner or a meal with friends. Mix and match toppings to create your ultimate fajita and celebrate...with more fajitas.

Makes 4 to 5 servings

- 1/3 cup lime juice
- 2 tablespoons soy sauce
- 2 tablespoons olive oil
- 3 cloves garlic, minced
- 1 teaspoon ground cumin
- 1 teaspoon chili powder
- 1 teaspoon smoked paprika
- 1/4 teaspoon salt
- 1/4 teaspoon freshly ground pepper
- 1 to 2 tablespoons mild vegetable oil, divided
- 1 recipe Basic Beef (page 16), sliced thin
- 2 medium white onions, sliced into thin half moons
- 1 large poblano pepper, seeds removed and sliced thin
- 2 to 3 bell peppers (pick two different colors)
- flour or corn tortillas, shredded cheese, guacamole, salsa, sour cream, cilantro, to serve

1. Combine the lime juice, soy sauce, olive oil, garlic, cumin, chili powder, paprika, salt, and pepper in a large shallow bowl or casserole dish. Adjust the seasoning with salt and pepper to taste.

2. Coat the sliced seitan in the mixture, cover, and refrigerate for at least 1 hour to marinate.

3. Heat the first tablespoon of vegetable oil in a large cast-iron skillet or pan over high heat. Add the seitan to the pan and cook for 2 to 3 minutes on each side, until edges feel firm and slightly crisp.

4. Lower the heat if the seitan is getting too dark. Remove from the pan, set aside on a plate, and cover with foil to keep warm.
5. Over medium-high heat, heat the remaining vegetable oil in the pan and add the onions, poblano pepper, and bell peppers.
6. Let the veggies begin to sizzle, stirring often for 2 to 3 minutes. Make sure you have some room in the pan, as you want them to sear slightly, not sauté, and stay crisp. Remove from the heat.
7. Serve with tortillas and a spread of your favorite toppings.

Israeli Salad with Chick'n and Tahini Sauce

Showcase your summer produce with this incredible salad. So refreshing and flavorful, it's the perfect solution to impress guests on hot summer days when you want to keep it simple.

Makes 4 servings

- ½ cup plain yogurt
- 1 teaspoon ground coriander
- 1 teaspoon paprika
- zest and juice of 2 lemons, to a total of ⅓ cup of juice, divided
- 3 cloves garlic, minced, divided
- ¼ cup olive oil, divided
- 1 recipe Chick'n Wings (page 29)
- ¼ cup tahini
- 3 extra-large tomatoes, seeded
- 1 English cucumber
- 1 small red onion
- 1 red bell pepper
- 1 yellow bell pepper
- ½ cup chopped parsley
- ½ cup chopped mint
- salt and freshly ground pepper to taste

1. In a large zip-top bag or a shallow bowl, whisk together the yogurt, coriander, paprika, 1 tablespoon lemon juice, ½ teaspoon lemon zest, 2 cloves minced garlic, and 1 tablespoon olive oil.
2. Add the Chick'n Wings and coat. Place the coated Chick'n and marinade in the fridge for 20 minutes.
3. Preheat the oven to 350°F and prep a baking sheet with parchment paper. Spread the Chick'n on the prepared sheet and bake for 20 to 25 minutes until golden, flipping halfway through. Let cool slightly.

4. In a small bowl, whisk together the tahini, 2 tablespoons lemon juice, remaining garlic, and a sprinkle of salt and pepper. Set aside.
5. In a large bowl, whisk together the remaining olive oil, remaining lemon juice and zest, and season to taste with salt and pepper.
6. Finely chop the tomatoes, cucumber, red onion, and bell peppers. Toss in the large bowl. Add the parsley and mint.
7. Slice each Chick'n Wing into thin slices. Serve several scoops of salad topped with sliced seitan and a drizzle of the tahini sauce.

Mega Sandwiches

These are the sandwiches I bring in the summer, to accompany us on weekend getaways. It's the best remedy for long car rides and hangry company outside of ice cream.

Makes 4 sandwiches

- ½ recipe Basic Seitan 2.0 (page 12), cut into long ½-inch-thick slices
- 3 tablespoons soy sauce
- 2 tablespoons olive oil, divided
- 1 tablespoon water
- 2 teaspoons lemon juice
- 1 teaspoon toasted sesame oil
- 3 cloves garlic, minced
- ½ teaspoon dried basil
- ½ teaspoon dried oregano
- ½ teaspoon onion powder
- sprinkle of freshly ground pepper
- soft but hearty sandwich bread
- Dijon mustard
- 1 (8-ounce) container hummus
- green leaf lettuce, rinsed and dried
- dill pickle sandwich slices, dried with a paper towel

1. Spread the seitan in a single layer in a baking dish.
2. In a small bowl, combine the soy sauce, 1 tablespoon of olive oil, water, lemon juice, sesame oil, garlic, basil, oregano, onion powder, and pepper.
3. Whisk to combine, pour over the seitan, and let sit for 20 minutes. Flip slices to coat thoroughly.
4. Heat the remaining 1 tablespoon olive oil in the bottom of a pan on medium heat. Add the seitan and cook until slightly browned, 5 to 10 minutes, flipping to cook both sides. Remove from the heat and let cool completely.

5. Divide pairs of bread slices. On one side of each sandwich, add a thin smear of mustard. On the other side, add a healthy spread of hummus.
6. Add a layer of seitan to the mustard side and place lettuce and pickle slices in the middle. Wrap each sandwich in plastic wrap and refrigerate for at least an hour before eating.

Meaty Tortellini Salad

If you make this recipes for a potluck, you will be the most popular person there, hands down.

Makes 4 to 5 servings

1 (8-ounce) bag rotini pasta

1 (10-ounce) package spinach-filled fresh tortellini

3 teaspoons Dijon mustard, divided

¼ cup olive oil, divided

2 to 3 tablespoons red wine vinegar

2 cloves garlic, crushed

1 tablespoon lemon juice

1 tablespoon water

½ recipe Chick'n Wings (page 29), cut into 1-inch chunks

½ teaspoon dried oregano

8 ounces crumbled goat cheese

½ cup fresh, julienned basil

1 cup cherry tomatoes, halved

salt and freshly ground pepper to taste

1. Cook the rotini and the tortellini according to the package directions.

2. While the pasta is cooking, in a small bowl, whisk together 2 teaspoons of the mustard, 2 tablespoons of the olive oil, and the red wine vinegar (more or less, to your desired tanginess), garlic, and a little salt and pepper. Adjust amounts to your desired taste.

3. In another small bowl, combine the remaining mustard, remaining olive oil, lemon juice, and water.

4. Heat a medium skillet on medium heat and add the Chick'n. Sprinkle with the lemon juice mixture and

the oregano and cook until lightly browned, about 5 minutes, stirring often. Set aside.

5. In a large bowl, combine the warm, drained rotini and tortellini.
6. Add the vinaigrette and toss to coat.
7. Add the goat cheese (some of it will melt into the pasta), then add the basil and tomatoes. Adjust the seasoning with salt and pepper to taste.
8. Serve with the Chick'n on top. Delicious warm or chilled.

Chopped Chick'n Ginger Salad

This salad is addictive and will quickly become a family favorite.

Makes 4 servings

- ½ recipe Chick'n Wings (page 29), chopped into bite-size pieces
- ¼ cup soy sauce
- 2 tablespoons grated fresh ginger
- 3 tablespoons mild vegetable oil, divided
- 1 tablespoon toasted sesame oil
- 1 teaspoon sriracha
- 2 tablespoons red wine vinegar
- 2 tablespoons lime juice
- salt and freshly ground pepper to taste
- 1 pound napa cabbage, cored, halved, and chopped into thin strips
- 2 medium carrots, peeled and cut into thin, 2-inch matchsticks
- 2/3 cup toasted slivered almonds
- ½ cup cilantro, chopped
- 3 green onions, green and white parts, chopped
- 2 teaspoons white sesame seeds, toasted
- 2 teaspoons black sesame seeds

1. Place the Chick'n Wings in a large bowl.
2. In a small bowl, mix together the soy sauce, ginger, 2 tablespoons of the vegetable oil, and the sesame oil, sriracha, red wine vinegar, and lime juice. Whisk together and add salt and pepper to taste.
3. Toss 3 tablespoons of the mixture with the Chick'n Wings. Reserve the remaining dressing in the fridge.

4. In a separate large bowl, toss together the cabbage and carrots. In a medium frying pan, heat the remaining 1 tablespoon vegetable oil on medium heat.

5. Add the Chick'n with any remaining juices and cook until browned, stirring often, about 5 to 7 minutes. Set aside to cool slightly.

6. Toss the cabbage with enough of the refrigerated dressing to coat.

7. Add the almonds, cilantro, green onions, and sesame seeds to the cabbage mixture and toss. Top with Chick'n and serve immediately.

Philly Cheese-Not-Steak Sandwiches

Originally from Pennsylvania, I could not resist a tip of the hat to this classic sandwich, piled high and smothered in cheese.

Makes 4 to 5 sandwiches

2 tablespoons mild vegetable oil, divided

2 medium green bell peppers, cored, seeded, and thinly sliced

1 medium yellow onion, thinly sliced

1 recipe Ribs (page 31), not seared, thinly sliced

8 ounces thinly sliced provolone cheese

4 to 5 hoagie rolls, split and toasted

salt and freshly ground pepper to taste

1. In a large frying pan over medium-high heat, heat 1 tablespoon of oil until shimmering.
2. Add the bell pepper and the onion. Stir to coat the veggies, and season with salt and pepper. Cook, stirring occasionally, until softened and starting to brown, about 5 minutes.
3. In a separate pan, heat the remaining 1 tablespoon oil and add the Ribs. Cook, stirring occasionally, until lightly browned, about 10 minutes. Reduce the heat to low.
4. Divide the Ribs into 4 to 5 piles roughly the size of the hoagie rolls. Place half of the veggies on top of each seitan portion.
5. Lay a portion of the cheese over each portion of steak and vegetables.

6. Cover the pan with a tight-fitting lid and let it heat through without stirring until the cheese has melted, about 3 minutes. Carefully transfer each pile into a roll and serve immediately.

Vegan variation: Substitute vegan cheese for the provolone, or a spread of a vegan cream cheese with crushed garlic and dried herbs mixed in.

Grilled Meaty Mushroom Kabobs

Serve kabobs over Fragrant Rice (page 186) for a heartier meal or with Creamy Slaw (page 107) for a light summer nosh.

Makes 6 to 8 kabobs

- 2 tablespoons honey or agave
- 2 tablespoons Dijon mustard
- 1 tablespoon balsamic vinegar
- 3 tablespoons mild vegetable oil, divided
- sprinkle of salt and freshly ground pepper
- ½ recipe Meaty-Spheres (page 47)
- 12 to 18 small white mushrooms, wiped clean and stems removed
- 1 medium green pepper, cored, seeded, cut into large chunks
- 1 medium yellow or red pepper, cored, seeded, cut into large chunks
- 1 medium white onion, cut into eighths, then cut into smaller chunks

1. Prepare the grill, if using coals, or heat a gas grill to a medium heat. Soak bamboo skewers in water (so they don't burn on the grill).
2. In a small bowl, whisk together the honey, mustard, balsamic vinegar, 1 tablespoon of the oil, and a sprinkle of salt and pepper. Set aside.
3. Prepare skewers by alternating the Meaty-Spheres, mushrooms, peppers, and onions. Leave about 1 inch of skewer on either end of each kabob. Set aside on a baking sheet and repeat.
4. Brush grill with some of the remaining oil. Place kabobs on the grill in a single layer and baste with the reserved marinade.

5. Cook for 2 minutes, then flip, basting the second side, and cook for 2 more minutes.

6. Continue flipping and basting until the edges of the onions are a little charred and look cooked but are still firm.

Italian Pasta Salad

Being from Minnesota, I pronounce this "EYE-talian" because, let's face it, this is not very authentic. But it is delicious, and that's all that really matters. The Sausage of the Summer (page 51) makes a really tasty meat in this salad.

Makes 4 to 6 servings

1 (16-ounce) package tricolored rotini pasta

1/4 cup olive oil

2 tablespoons white wine vinegar

2 tablespoons water

1 to 2 teaspoons honey or agave

juice of 1 lemon (about 2 to 3 tablespoons)

1/4 teaspoon garlic powder

1/4 teaspoon dried basil

1/4 teaspoon dried oregano

pinch of red pepper flakes

sprinkle of salt and freshly ground pepper to taste

1/2 recipe Sausage of the Summer, cut into thin half moons

1 cup marinated artichokes, drained and chopped

1 cup good-quality black olives

1 cup good-quality green olives

1/3 cup pepperoncini, drained and chopped

1 seedless cucumber, thinly sliced

1/2 large red onion, diced

1/2 cup Italian parsley, chopped

1 cup grated Parmesan cheese

1. Bring a large pot of water to a boil and cook the pasta according to the package directions. Drain, rinse in cold water, and set aside.

2. In a jar with a lid, combine the olive oil, vinegar, water, honey or agave, lemon juice, garlic powder, basil,

oregano, and red pepper flakes, and tightly close the lid. Shake well to combine. Taste and adjust the seasoning with salt and pepper.

3. In a large bowl, place the Sausage of the Summer, artichokes, olives, pepperoncini, cucumber, red onion, and parsley.

4. Add the pasta on top. Drizzle with the dressing and toss to combine.

5. Add more olive oil, salt and pepper to taste, if needed. Top with grated Parmesan.

6. Chill for at least 1 to 2 hours before serving.

Vegan variation: Omit the Parmesan.

Special Occasion Seitan

Sometimes a slab of faux ribs or some chick'n cutlets are just not quite enough. Sometimes, you have to bring in the big guns.

These are recipes that take a little longer. There are more steps. There is more prep. But that's okay—they aren't scary. They just require a little extra time. Perfect for lazy Sundays capped off with decadent dinners or for holidays and special occasions when you really want to go all out.

Savory Seitan Tart

This elegant tart is delicious in flavor and impressive in presentation. While slightly time-consuming, it will truly shine as the centerpiece of any table.

Makes 5 to 6 servings

- 1 recipe Basic Tart Crust (page 133)
- 2 tablespoons olive oil, divided
- 1 small white onion, chopped
- 2 cloves garlic, minced
- 2 cups cremini mushrooms, rinsed and sliced
- 2 (15-ounce) cans chickpeas, drained and rinsed
- white wine, as needed
- ¼ cup nutritional yeast
- 1 tablespoon finely chopped fresh thyme
- 1 tablespoon finely chopped fresh rosemary
- 2 tablespoons soy sauce
- 1 tablespoon balsamic vinegar
- 3 Italian Sausages (page 34), cut into large chunks
- 2 tablespoons unsalted butter
- 3 to 4 cups pearl onions, peeled
- sprinkle of sugar

1. Prepare the tart crust. Wrap in plastic wrap and let chill in the refrigerator.
2. In a large skillet, heat one tablespoon of olive oil, then sauté the white onion until translucent, about 10 minutes. Add garlic and cook until fragrant, about 1 minute.
3. Add the mushrooms and cook until they release their liquid. Drain off any liquid.

4. Add the chickpeas and sauté for about 10 minutes over medium heat, stirring often and adding splashes of wine to deglaze the pan as needed.

5. Add the nutritional yeast and herbs and stir to coat.

6. Add soy sauce and balsamic vinegar. Stir to combine, then transfer the mixture to a food processor.

7. Process, adding more wine as needed and scraping down the sides of the processor to make a mixture like a thick pâté.

8. Pulse in the sausages so they are chunkily incorporated. Set aside.

9. In a large pan, melt the butter over medium heat. Add the remaining olive oil and pearl onions. Sprinkle with a little sugar and cook, stirring often, until the onions are translucent and they begin to caramelize, about 15 minutes. Add splashes of wine as needed to deglaze the pan.

10. Preheat the oven to 400°F. Remove the pie crust from the fridge. Press the crust into the bottom and sides of a 12-inch tart pan. You may not use all of the crust, depending on how thick you make it.

11. Spread the chickpea mixture into the crust and smooth with a spatula. Top with the pearl onions and press them gently into the tart.

12. Bake, covered with tin foil, for about 45 minutes, then remove the foil and bake for an additional 10 to 15 minutes, or until the top is set. Let the tart sit for 10 to 15 minutes before serving.

13. You can easily prep this recipe the night before and refrigerate it, then bake the day of serving. If you're baking it directly from the fridge, you might need to add 10 minutes to the bake time.

Basic Tart Crust

This simple tart crust will happily support sweet or savory fare.

Makes one 9- to 10- inch crust

2½ cups unbleached all-purpose flour

1 tablespoon sugar

¼ teaspoon salt

1 cup cold unsalted butter, cut into chunks

¼ to ½ cup cold water

1. In a food processor, combine the flour, sugar, and salt. Pulse a few times to blend.
2. Add the butter and pulse the mixture until it becomes a coarse meal.
3. Slowly add the water, 1 tablespoon at a time, until a dough comes together.
4. Press the dough into a disc. Wrap in plastic wrap and refrigerate for at least 1 hour before using.
5. Alternatively, combine the flour, sugar, and salt in a bowl. Using a pastry cutter or fork, blend in the butter until mixture becomes a coarse meal. Add water 2 tablespoons at a time and quickly mix until a dough comes together.

Lazy Sunday Meatloaf

Tempeh adds a little nuttiness to this loaf, giving it a lovely texture and flavor. Serve with roasted potatoes, Miso Mushroom Gravy (page 179), and a big green salad for a hearty and wholesome Sunday supper.

Makes 4 to 5 servings

- 2 cups vital wheat gluten
- 1 teaspoon paprika
- 1 teaspoon dried thyme
- 1 teaspoon dried sage
- sprinkle of salt and freshly ground pepper
- 1 ½ cups low-sodium vegetable broth
- 3 tablespoons soy sauce
- 2 tablespoons tomato paste
- 2 tablespoons olive oil
- 1 tablespoon molasses
- 3 cloves garlic
- 8 ounces tempeh, crumbled
- ketchup (optional)

1. Preheat the oven to 325°F. Line a 9 x 5-inch loaf pan with tin foil, two layers overlapping in either direction, with enough of an overhang that you'll be able to wrap it over the loaf.

2. In a large bowl, whisk together the wheat gluten, paprika, thyme, sage, and a sprinkle of salt and pepper. Set aside.

3. In a food processor, blend together the vegetable broth, soy sauce, tomato paste, olive oil, and molasses until smooth. Pulse in the garlic and crumbled tempeh until it's a fairly smooth, but slightly chunky, consistency.

4. Make a well in the middle of the dry ingredients and pour in the wet ingredients. Stir to combine as much as possible, then use your hands to incorporate.
5. Gently knead until a cohesive dough comes together. It might be dense, but should be somewhat pliable.
6. Shape into a loaf and press into the prepared pan. Cover well with the overhanging tin foil.
7. Bake for 90 minutes. If you like ketchup on your meatloaf, peel back the tin foil after 75 minutes, add the ketchup, and bake, uncovered, for the remaining 15 minutes.
8. Let rest for 10 to 15 minutes before cutting and serving.

Slow Cooker Roast

This takes some time, but it's well worth it. The resulting roast is tender and flavorful, and your house will smell like foodie heaven. The cheesecloth does all the work, giving your roast the best flavor possible.

Makes 4 to 6 servings

For the roast:

2 cups vital wheat gluten

¼ cup unbleached all-purpose flour

1 teaspoon paprika

1 tablespoon ground sage

1 tablespoon dried oregano

sprinkle of salt and freshly ground pepper

1½ cups low-sodium vegetable broth

3 tablespoons olive oil

1 tablespoon tomato paste

1 large white or yellow onion, halved and cut into large half moons

1 stalk celery

2 cloves garlic

For the broth:

4 cups low-sodium vegetable broth

3 tablespoons soy sauce

1 tablespoon toasted sesame oil

4 large red or Yukon potatoes, rinsed, skin on, chopped into 6 large chunks each

4 large carrots, cut into 2-inch chunks

1. In a large bowl, combine the wheat gluten, flour, paprika, sage, oregano, salt, and pepper.
2. In a food processor, combine the vegetable broth, olive oil, and tomato paste, and blend to combine.

3. Add half of the onion, celery, and garlic, and pulse until finely chopped into the liquid. Add the wet mixture to the dry mixture and combine well to make a nice loaf.

4. Unroll a piece of cheesecloth twice as big as the roast. Lay the roast on one end and roll to cover twice. Secure the ends with kitchen twine.

5. For the broth, in a food processor, incorporate the 4 cups of vegetable broth, the soy sauce, and the sesame oil.

6. Place the roast in the bottom of the slow cooker and surround with the remaining onion, celery, and garlic, and the potatoes and carrots. Pour in enough broth mixture to just cover the roast.

7. Cook on low for 6 to 8 hours, flipping the roast once. The roast should feel yielding but firm (not squishy) in the middle when poked. Remove from the cheesecloth before serving alongside the vegetables.

Seitan-Tucken

Why should meat eaters have all the fun? Rather than doing unmentionably gross things to various fowl, this Seitan-Tucken is an amazing project for your next big holiday dinner. Time-consuming? Sure. Worth the effort? Absolutely. As early ahead as the night before serving, you can make the Tucken up to the point where the seitan is wrapped around it, then wrap well in plastic wrap and refrigerate. Bake it the day of.

Don't get scared off by how long the recipe is. Read it through once or twice before starting to make sure you know the steps, then take it one piece at a time. It's much easier than it looks.

Sweet, maple-infused butternut squash is the core of this roast, which is wrapped in smoky tempeh and then encased in herbed seitan to impress your guests' taste buds as well as their cruelty-free sensibilities. Pair with Apple Sausage Stuffing (page 188) and your other holiday fixings for an incredible celebratory meal.

Makes 6 to 8 servings

For the butternut squash layer:

- 1 small butternut squash, about 2 pounds
- 1 teaspoon mild vegetable oil
- 3 tablespoons maple syrup, divided

For the tempeh layer:

- 2 tablespoons soy sauce
- 1 to 2 tablespoons water
- 2 teaspoons mild vegetable oil
- 1 to 2 teaspoons liquid smoke
- 16 ounces tempeh, crumbled
- salt and freshly ground pepper to taste
- 1/4 cup vital wheat gluten
- sprinkle of water

For the seitan layer:

2 cups vital wheat gluten

¼ cup unbleached all-purpose flour

2 teaspoons paprika (sweet, if possible)

1 teaspoon dried thyme

1 teaspoon dried sage

1 teaspoon dried tarragon

sprinkle of salt and freshly ground pepper

1½ cups low-sodium vegetable broth

½ cup navy or cannellini beans, drained and rinsed

3 cloves garlic, chopped

2 tablespoons soy sauce

2 tablespoons Dijon mustard

2 tablespoons olive oil

1 teaspoon toasted sesame oil

1. For the butternut squash layer, peel the butternut squash before cutting in half lengthwise. Scoop out and discard the seeds.

2. Cut into long, ½-inch-thick strips. In a large skillet, bring ½ inch of water to a simmer over medium heat.

3. Add the butternut squash in a single layer, cover, and cook until just tender, 2 to 3 minutes. Drain the water.

4. Add the vegetable oil and 2 tablespoons of the maple syrup, gently stirring to coat. Lower the heat to medium-low and cook, stirring often, until the edges of the squash are gently browned or caramelized, 15 minutes.

5. Remove the squash from the pan and set aside. Reserve the remaining 1 tablespoon maple syrup.

6. For the tempeh, in the same large skillet, combine the soy sauce, water, vegetable oil, and liquid smoke. Whisk to combine, then add the crumbled tempeh.

7. Cook over medium heat, stirring often, until the liquid is absorbed and the tempeh is lightly browned. Check for flavor. Add more liquid smoke, if desired, and season with salt and pepper.
8. Gently mash to break up large clumps, then set aside to cool. Once slightly cooled, sprinkle with the wheat gluten and stir to combine.
9. Add a little sprinkle of water and stir to combine, making a lumpy, thick mixture that should slightly stick together. The little bit of gluten will help hold the tempeh together.
10. For the seitan, in a large bowl, combine the wheat gluten, flour, paprika, thyme, sage, tarragon, and a sprinkle of salt and pepper.
11. In a food processor, combine the vegetable stock, beans, garlic, soy sauce, mustard, olive oil, and sesame oil, and blend until smooth.
12. Add the wet mixture to the dry and combine, kneading gently into a smooth dough.
13. To assemble, preheat oven to 350°F. Prepare 2 large pieces of tin foil, about 18 inches long each. Have cooking twine ready.
14. On a piece of waxed paper on top of a baking sheet, press the tempeh into an 8 x 10-inch rectangle, making sure it's packed firmly. Place in freezer to chill for 10 to 15 minutes—this will make it easier to handle.
15. Remove the tempeh from the freezer and place strips of cooled butternut squash in the center. Leave 1 inch of tempeh exposed on all four sides, and bundle enough

squash together to make a 2-inch core of butternut squash. Baste with the remaining maple syrup.

16. Using the waxed paper to help you, gently roll up the tempeh, tucking the remaining 1 inch over the edges of the squash. You might need to return it to the freezer for a few minutes to make it easier. Work carefully—if it breaks up a little, that's okay, just press it back together. Wrap in plastic wrap and return to freezer for 20 minutes to chill.

17. On a clean surface, roll out the seitan into a 10 x 12-inch rectangle. If it tears a little, that's okay. Press the pieces back together.

18. Remove tempeh roll from the freezer. Gently remove the plastic wrap and roll onto one long end of the seitan.

19. Fold the edges of the seitan in and roll up tightly, wrapping the tempeh/butternut squash layers in.

20. Place seam-side down and use cooking twine to secure the loaf several times around. Wrap the loaf firmly in the prepared tin foil, using more if needed, twisting the ends to secure.

21. Place on a baking sheet and bake for 90 minutes to 2 hours, flipping the loaf halfway through cooking. Use tongs to squeeze the loaf in the middle to determine doneness. It should yield slightly but feel firm, not squishy.

22. Let the loaf cool for 30 minutes in the foil before serving.

Seitan and Mushrooms en Croûte

Tender seitan and toothsome mushrooms, wrapped in a puff pastry and baked to golden perfection—it's mealtime bliss, seriously. Serve with Miso Mushroom Gravy (page 179) to take it all the way.

Makes 4 to 6 servings

2 teaspoons mild vegetable oil

2 large portobello mushrooms, stems removed, gills scraped out, wiped clean, and roughly chopped

1 heaping cup sliced white or cremini mushrooms, wiped clean and roughly chopped

2 cups vital wheat gluten

¼ cup nutritional yeast

1 teaspoon dried thyme

1 teaspoon dried sage

1 teaspoon garlic powder

½ teaspoon onion powder

sprinkle of salt and freshly ground pepper

1½ cups low-sodium vegetable broth

2 tablespoons soy sauce

¼ cup olive oil, divided

2 cloves garlic, crushed

1 sheet puff pastry, defrosted but chilled in refrigerator

1. Preheat the oven to 350°F. Ready 2 large sheets of tin foil, about 16 to 18 inches long, and a baking sheet.

2. In a large sauté pan, heat the vegetable oil over medium heat. Add the chopped mushrooms and cook, stirring often, until they release their liquid, about 5 to 10 minutes. Drain the liquid and set the mushrooms aside to cool.

3. In a large bowl, combine the wheat gluten, nutritional yeast, thyme, sage, garlic powder, onion powder, salt, and pepper.
4. In a medium bowl, whisk together the vegetable broth, soy sauce, 2 tablespoons of the olive oil, and the garlic.
5. Add the mushrooms, then add the wet mixture to the dry, stirring to combine. Gently knead and shape into a loaf about 8 to 10 inches long.
6. Wrap in foil tightly, twisting the ends to secure, place on the baking sheet, and bake for 40 minutes. Remove from the oven and loosen the tin foil, letting the loaf cool slightly. Increase the oven temperature to 375°F.
7. Unfold the puff pastry on a clean surface and roll out to 14 inches long. Remove the foil from the seitan loaf and place it at one edge of the puff pastry. Fold the ends over and roll the loaf to encase it in the pastry.
8. Place seam-side down on the baking sheet and score the pastry several times. Brush with the remaining 2 tablespoons of olive oil and bake for 30 more minutes, until the puff pastry is golden.
9. Let cool for 15 minutes before slicing and serving.

Vegan variation: Pepperidge Farms brand puff pastry is dairy-free.

Dinner

Your seitan should be properly showcased—enjoyed by the belly as well as the eyes. Whether it's a special occasion meal or a comfort food classic, these recipes pack in flavor and texture, so your seitan masterpiece will be enjoyed by meat eaters and veggie eaters alike!

Kielbasa and Kraut

Look for the good sauerkraut, in the grocery store's refrigerated section, not the stuff from a can. You'll be happy that you did.

Makes 4 servings

- 2 tablespoons mild vegetable oil
- 4 medium red potatoes, peeled and cut into ½-inch slices
- ½ teaspoon caraway seeds
- 1 small white onion, cut into half moons
- 1 recipe Kielbasa (page 38), cut into ½-inch cubes
- 1 (16-ounce) package sauerkraut, rinsed and well drained
- salt and freshly ground pepper to taste

1. In a large skillet, heat the oil over medium-high heat. Cook the potatoes until slightly browned, about 5 minutes.
2. Add the caraway seeds, being careful as they might pop.
3. Stir in the onion, lower the heat to medium, and sauté for 3 to 4 minutes or until the onion is tender.
4. Add the sausage and sauerkraut. Cook, uncovered, over medium-low heat for 10 minutes, until heated through, stirring occasionally. Taste and then add salt and pepper, if needed.

Baked Ziti with Sausage

This recipe has a couple of steps to get everything in the casserole, but it's totally worth it—the end result is hearty, homemade Italian food. Always worth the effort.

Makes 5 to 6 generous servings

- 3 tablespoons olive oil, divided
- 4 Italian Sausages (page 34), sliced into ½-inch coins
- 4 cups uncooked ziti pasta
- 2 large zucchini, cut into ½-inch half moons
- 1 medium yellow onion, chopped
- 3 cloves garlic, minced
- ½ cup red wine
- 1 (28-ounce) can crushed plum tomatoes
- ⅓ cup black or kalamata olives, chopped
- 2½ cups shredded mozzarella cheese
- salt and freshly ground pepper to taste
- ½ cup grated Parmesan cheese

1. In a large skillet, heat 1 tablespoon of the oil over medium heat. Add the sausage coins and cook until browned, about 5 to 8 minutes, stirring often. Transfer the sausages to a large bowl.
2. In a large pot, prepare the ziti according to the package directions. Drain and rinse with cold water and set aside.
3. Using the same skillet that you cooked the sausage in, heat 1 more tablespoon of the oil over medium heat. Add the zucchini and cook until tender and lightly browned. Transfer to the bowl with the sausage.
4. In the same skillet, heat remaining 1 tablespoon oil over medium heat. Add the onion and cook until slightly

translucent, about 3 minutes. Add the garlic and cook until fragrant, about 1 minute.

5. Pour the wine into the skillet, increase the heat to medium-high, and stir to combine. Add the tomatoes and cook until the liquid is slightly reduced, then lower the heat. Simmer for 10 minutes.

6. Preheat oven to 400°F. Lightly grease a 3-quart baking dish.

7. To the bowl with the sausage mixture, add the cooked pasta, olives, 2 cups of the mozzarella, and the tomato sauce. Season to taste with salt and pepper. Stir to combine.

8. Transfer the mixture to the prepared baking dish. Sprinkle with the remaining mozzarella and the Parmesan cheese.

9. Cover with tin foil and bake for 25 to 30 minutes. Uncover and bake for 5 more minutes, or until lightly browned. Let stand 5 minutes before serving.

Spicy Peanut Noodles

Everything is better with peanut butter and these delicious noodles are no exception. This is a hearty dinner that can come together quickly, which is always a weeknight lifesaver.

Makes 4 to 5 servings

- 1 tablespoon mild vegetable oil
- ½ teaspoon toasted sesame oil
- 1 inch fresh ginger, peeled and grated
- ½ recipe Chick'n Wings (page 29), cut into quarters
- 8 ounces buckwheat soba noodles
- 2 carrots, julienned or cut into matchsticks
- 1 red bell pepper, seeded and diced small
- 1 recipe Spicy Peanut Sauce (page 60)
- 3 to 4 green onions, chopped into ¼-inch pieces
- sesame seeds, for garnish

1. In a large skillet, heat the vegetable oil and sesame oil over medium heat. Add the ginger and cook until fragrant, about 2 minutes.
2. Add the Chick'n Wings and cook until golden, about 10 minutes, stirring often. Remove from the heat and set aside.
3. Cook the buckwheat noodles according to the package directions.
4. While the noodles are cooking, add the carrots and bell pepper to the skillet with the Chick'n. Heat over low heat, covered, for about 5 minutes, until the carrots and bell pepper are vibrant in color and heated through.

5. In a separate skillet, heat the Spicy Peanut Sauce. Add the cooked, drained noodles and toss to coat. Top with the Chick'n and veggies and toss.
6. Serve each helping with a sprinkle of green onions and sesame seeds.

Chick'n Fried Steak

Chicken Fried Steak contains no chicken, and this Chick'n Fried Steak contains neither chicken nor steak, yet that doesn't stop it from being a crispy, tasty treat—serve on a bed of Ultimate Mashed Potatoes (page 178) and smothered with Miso Mushroom Gravy (page 179). With all the flavor going on, it's likely that the meat eaters among us won't even notice it's seitan.

Makes 6 to 8 servings

For the wet mixture:

- 1/3 cup water
- 2 tablespoons Dijon mustard
- 3 tablespoons unbleached all-purpose flour

For the dry mixture:

- 1 cup unbleached all-purpose flour
- 1 teaspoon garlic powder
- 1/2 teaspoon paprika
- 1/2 teaspoon salt
- 1/2 teaspoon freshly ground pepper
- 1 recipe Ribs (page 31), not seared, halved lengthwise
- vegetable, peanut, or canola oil, enough for about 1 inch in a large skillet

1. For the wet mix, in a shallow bowl, whisk together the water, mustard, and 3 tablespoons of flour into a slurry.
2. For the dry mixture, in another shallow bowl, whisk together the flour, garlic powder, paprika, salt, and pepper.
3. Dip each piece of seitan Ribs into the wet mixture, then coat with the dry mixture. Set aside on a clean plate or piece of waxed paper. Repeat with the remaining pieces.

4. Heat about ½ inch of oil in a large skillet over medium-high, until a little bit of the steak coating sizzles and browns.

5. Add the seitan in one layer (you may need to cook in two batches) and cook until golden, about 2 minutes, before flipping over and cooking the other side until golden, about 2 more minutes. Remove from the oil and drain on a plate lined with paper towels.

Italian Sausages and Peppers

Fragrant, tangy, and hearty, this meal is quick to make, but impressive to serve. Serve over polenta or rice.

Makes 4 to 5 servings

- 2 tablespoons olive oil
- 1 large white onion, sliced into thin half moons
- 4 cloves garlic, crushed
- 1 recipe Italian Sausages (page 34), each cut into 2 to 3 pieces
- 1 tablespoon dried oregano
- 2 large Roma tomatoes, cut into 6 pieces each
- 1 (15-ounce) can whole tomatoes
- ½ cup red wine
- 1 green bell pepper, seeded and cut into thin half moons
- 1 red or yellow bell pepper, seeded and cut into thin half moons

1. Heat the olive oil in a large skillet over medium heat. Sauté the onion until translucent, about 5 minutes, then add the garlic and cook until fragrant, about 5 minutes.
2. Add the sausage pieces to the skillet. Cook until lightly browned, stirring often, about 5 minutes.
3. Add the oregano and stir to coat.
4. Add the Roma tomatoes and the canned tomatoes, then the wine. Bring to a boil, then lower to a simmer. Cover and cook for about 25 minutes, stirring occasionally, adding the bell peppers in the last 10 minutes of cooking.

Brinner Bake

Brinner—breakfast for dinner—is, by far, the best meal (after brunch, that is). If you're going to go crazy and make this for breakfast you can prepare it the night before, cover and refrigerate, and pop it in the oven for an extra 5 to 10 minutes in the morning.

Makes 4 to 6 servings

1 (12-ounce) loaf of sourdough or French bread, chopped into cubes

1 recipe Smoky Maple Breakfast Links (page 45), each chopped into 3 to 4 pieces

8 eggs

2½ cups milk of choice

½ cup sugar

1 tablespoon vanilla extract

2 teaspoons ground cinnamon

maple syrup, to serve

1. Preheat the oven to 350°F. Grease a 9 x 13-inch pan.
2. Fill the pan with the cubed bread and breakfast sausage chunks, and toss to combine.
3. In a large bowl, whisk together the eggs, milk, sugar, vanilla, and cinnamon. Pour evenly over the bread and sausage.
4. Cover the pan with plastic wrap and let sit for at least 30 minutes.
5. Bake for 45 to 55 minutes, until the edges are crusty and the casserole gently yields when pushed.
6. Serve with maple syrup.

Vegan variation: Replace the eggs with 8 ounces of pureed silken tofu. Increase the milk slightly if needed.

Not Beef with Broccoli

Perfectly cooked broccoli and sweet carrots, coated with a layer of garlicky brown sauce, accented with chunks of beef, and served on a bed of rice—could anything be more delicious?

Makes 4 to 5 servings

- ⅓ cup soy sauce, divided
- ¼ cup rice wine, divided
- 2 teaspoons cornstarch
- ½ cup low-sodium vegetable broth
- 1 tablespoon evaporated cane sugar
- 1 teaspoon sesame oil
- 3 cloves garlic, minced
- 1 tablespoon finely minced fresh ginger
- 1½ cups uncooked white or brown rice
- 3 tablespoons mild vegetable oil, divided
- 6 cups broccoli florets
- ⅓ cup water
- 2 cups sliced carrots, cut diagonally, ¼ inch thick
- ½ recipe Basic Beef (page 16), cut into 1 x 2-inch strips, each ¼ inch thick

1. Reserve 2 tablespoons of the soy sauce and 2 tablespoons of the rice wine and set aside in a small bowl.
2. Meanwhile, combine the remaining soy sauce with the cornstarch and whisk with a fork until the cornstarch is dissolved. Add the remaining rice wine, and the vegetable broth, sugar, and sesame oil. Stir and set aside.
3. Combine the garlic and ginger in a small bowl and set aside.
4. Prepare the rice according to the package directions.

5. Once the rice has been cooking for a bit, heat 1 tablespoon of the vegetable oil in a large saucepan or wok over high heat. Add the broccoli and stir-fry for 30 seconds, then add the water.

6. Cover the pan and lower the heat to medium. Steam the broccoli for 1 minute before adding the carrot slices. Cook 1 minute longer, until the broccoli and carrots are brightly colored, then transfer to a bowl.

7. Drain the water and return the pan to the heat. Increase the heat to high and add another tablespoon of the vegetable oil.

8. Add half of the seitan and half of the reserved soy sauce/rice wine so that it is in a single layer, and cook without moving until the seitan is seared, about 1 minute. Transfer to a plate.

9. Lower the heat to medium. Repeat with the remaining oil, the other half of the seitan, and the remaining soy sauce/rice wine. Transfer the seitan to the plate.

10. Add the garlic and ginger and cook for about 30 seconds, until fragrant.

11. Pour the prepared sauce into the pan and bring to a boil. Return the seitan, broccoli, and carrots to the pan, tossing and stirring constantly until heated through and the sauce is lightly thickened, about 1 minute.

12. Transfer the stir-fry to a serving platter and serve with the rice.

Summer Chick'n Primavera

This meal provides hearty protein while giving summer's bounty a stage to showcase its splendor. This is a great recipe to improvise with whatever veggies you're harvesting this week.

Makes 4 servings

- 16 ounces penne pasta
- 2 tablespoons olive oil, divided
- ½ recipe Chick'n Wings (page 29), cut into bite-size pieces
- 1 clove garlic, minced
- 1 cup small chopped broccoli florets
- 2 carrots, peeled and sliced diagonally
- ½ cup chopped red onion
- ½ red bell pepper, seeded and sliced into 1-inch-long strips
- 1 medium zucchini, sliced
- ½ cup chopped tomatoes
- 1 teaspoon chopped fresh oregano
- ¼ cup chopped fresh basil
- 1 tablespoon butter
- ⅔ cup grated Parmesan cheese
- salt and freshly ground pepper to taste

1. Cook the pasta according to the package directions.
2. While the pasta is cooking, heat 1 tablespoon of the olive oil in a large skillet and add the Chick'n Wings. Cook until golden on each side, about 4 to 5 minutes on each side. Transfer to a plate.
3. Heat the remaining 1 tablespoon oil and the garlic over medium heat until fragrant, about a minute.
4. Add the broccoli, carrots, and onion, and stir-fry for about 3 minutes.

5. Add the bell pepper and zucchini, and stir-fry another 2 minutes. Add the tomatoes, oregano, and basil. Cook another 1 to 2 minutes, until the tomatoes are tender. Add the seitan and cook until heated through.
6. Drain the cooked pasta and place in a large bowl. Toss the pasta with the butter to coat.
7. Add the veggies and seitan to the pasta. Add the Parmesan cheese and lightly toss, adding salt and pepper to taste, if needed.

Seitan Marsala

This elegant meal is perfect served over Ultimate Mashed Potatoes (page 178), polenta, couscous, or any other starch your heart desires.

Makes 4 servings

- 2 tablespoons olive oil, divided
- 1 small yellow onion, chopped
- 8 ounces cremini mushrooms, thinly sliced
- 2 cloves garlic, minced
- 1/4 cup unbleached all-purpose flour, divided
- 3/4 cup Marsala wine
- 1 1/2 cups low-sodium vegetable broth
- 1/2 teaspoon dried thyme
- salt and freshly ground pepper to taste
- 2 tablespoons cornstarch
- 1/2 recipe Chick'n Wings (page 29), each chunk cut in half
- mashed potatoes or polenta, to serve

1. In a large skillet, heat 1 tablespoon of the oil. When it smells fragrant, add the onion and mushrooms.
2. When the onion starts to look translucent and the mushrooms start giving off their juices, add the garlic and stir for another 30 seconds, until fragrant.
3. Add 2 tablespoons of the flour and stir to coat. After about a minute, add the wine to deglaze the pan. Scrape up any crusty bits from the pan. This will add flavor to the sauce. Remove onion, mushrooms, and garlic and set aside.
4. Add the vegetable broth and thyme. Bring to a boil for a minute and then lower to a simmer. Cook until the liquid is reduced to about half the volume, about 10 minutes.

5. Return the onions and mushrooms to the pan and stir to combine. Add salt and pepper to taste.
6. In the meantime, combine the remaining flour and the cornstarch in a large zip-top bag. Toss the Chick'n Wings in the mixture to lightly coat.
7. In a separate pan, heat the remaining 1 tablespoon oil on medium-high. Add the seitan and cook until golden and crispy before flipping, about 4 minutes on each side.
8. Arranged the cooked seitan over mashed potatoes or polenta and top with the mushroom sauce.

Work Night Scratch Spaghetti

Weeknights can be a bear: There just aren't enough hours in the day to make spaghetti sauce from scratch—or are there? This tasty sauce comes together easily and you can play with this recipe to use different kinds of seitan—omit the Ground Not-Beef and use Meaty-Spheres (page 47) or Italian Sausages (page 34).

Makes 4 servings

- 2 tablespoons olive oil
- 1 medium white onion, chopped
- 3 cloves garlic, crushed
- ½ recipe Ground Not-Beef (page 26)
- 1 teaspoon dried oregano
- 1 teaspoon dried basil
- 1 tablespoon dried parsley
- ½ teaspoon garlic powder
- 1 (28-ounce) can crushed tomatoes
- 1 (15-ounce) can tomato sauce
- 1 tablespoon evaporated cane sugar
- red pepper flakes to taste
- salt and freshly ground pepper to taste
- ¼ to ½ cup water
- 1 (16-ounce) package spaghetti

1. Heat the oil in a large skillet over medium heat. Sauté the onion until translucent, about 5 minutes.
2. Add the garlic and Ground Not-Beef and cook until garlic is fragrant, about 2 minutes.
3. Add the oregano, basil, parsley, and garlic powder, and coat the onion mixture with the herbs. Add the tomatoes with their juices, tomato sauce, and sugar.
4. Bring to a boil and then taste. Add salt and pepper to taste and red pepper flakes, if using.

5. Cover and lower the heat to medium-low and simmer for 30 minutes. Add water, if needed, if sauce gets too thick.
6. While the sauce is simmering, prepare the spaghetti according to package directions. Serve the sauce over the hot spaghetti.

Sweet and Sour Chick'n

Tangy and chewy, this classic dish will be a welcome revival in your kitchen.

Makes 4 servings

- 1 1/2 cups uncooked white or brown rice
- 3/4 cup sugar
- 1/2 cup apple cider vinegar
- 2 tablespoons soy sauce
- 1 teaspoon garlic powder
- 1/2 teaspoon onion powder
- 1/4 cup ketchup
- 1/4 cup plus 1 tablespoon cornstarch, divided
- 2 tablespoons water
- 1 recipe Chick'n Wings (page 29), cut into 1-inch pieces
- 2 tablespoons mild vegetable oil
- 1 red bell pepper, seeded and finely sliced
- 1 white onion, thinly sliced

1. Cook the rice according to the package directions.
2. Prepare the sauce by mixing together the sugar, vinegar, soy sauce, garlic powder, onion powder, and ketchup in a medium saucepan. Heat on medium and bring to a boil.
3. In a small bowl, whisk together 1 tablespoon of the cornstarch with the water, then whisk into the sauce. Bring back to a boil and lower to a simmer until slightly thickened, about 2 to 3 minutes.
4. Toss the Chick'n Wings with the remaining 1/4 cup cornstarch in a zip-top bag or large bowl.
5. Heat the oil a large sauté pan over medium heat. Add the Chick'n and cook until golden, about 5 minutes. Add the bell pepper and onion. Continue to sauté over

medium heat until the onions are tender, about 5 to 10 minutes.

6. Add the sauce to the Chick'n and peppers, and bring to a simmer. Serve warm with the cooked rice.

Broccoli Cheddar Chick'n Skillet

This is hearty, comfort food at its finest. When cold weather strikes, this recipe will be there to soothe the soul and nourish the tummy.

Makes 4 to 5 servings

- 2 tablespoons olive oil, divided
- 1 small white onion, chopped
- 4 cloves garlic, minced
- 1 recipe Basic Chick'n (page 14), cubed
- 3 tablespoons unbleached all-purpose flour
- 3 cups low-sodium vegetable broth
- 1 tablespoon soy sauce
- ¾ cup uncooked basmati rice
- 1 tablespoon unsalted butter
- 3 cups broccoli florets
- 1 cup shredded cheddar cheese
- salt and freshly ground pepper to taste

1. Heat 1 tablespoon of the olive oil in a large skillet with high sides. Add the onion and cook until translucent, about 5 minutes.

2. Add the garlic and cubed Chick'n, lowering the heat to medium-low. Cook until the Chick'n starts to brown a bit. Season with salt and pepper to taste.

3. Sprinkle with flour to coat and add a splash of the vegetable broth. Cook until the flour has a slightly toasted smell, but doesn't brown.

4. Add ¼ cup of the broth and mix to help dissolve the flour. Add the rest of the broth, soy sauce, and rice. Bring to a boil then lower to a simmer and cover.

5. Cook until the rice is fully cooked, about 15 minutes. Stir in the butter to melt, and adjust the seasoning with salt and pepper to taste.

6. Add the broccoli florets and half the cheese, and continue cooking for 3 to 4 more minutes, until the broccoli softens a bit.

7. Remove from the heat, sprinkle with the remaining cheese, and cover, waiting for the cheese to melt.

Vegan variation: Substitute non-dairy margarine for the butter and non-dairy cheese for the cheddar. Alternatively, you can cut in half a block of non-dairy cream cheese with 1 tablespoon mild, light-colored miso and stir until they melt down before adding the broccoli.

Hearty Macaroni Bake

This is mac 'n cheese for grownups. With a layer of tomatoes on the bottom and a richly flavored sauce, no one can accuse you of being a kid.

Makes 4 to 5 servings

- 1 tablespoon olive oil
- 1 small yellow onion, minced
- ½ recipe Chick'n Wings (page 29), cubed
- 1 (28-ounce) can diced tomatoes, drained
- 1 (16-ounce) bag rotini pasta
- 3 tablespoons unsalted butter
- ¼ cup unbleached all-purpose flour
- 3 cups milk of choice, divided
- 2 teaspoons Dijon mustard
- 1 teaspoon dried basil
- 1 teaspoon dried oregano
- 1 teaspoon garlic powder
- ½ teaspoon salt
- 4 cups shredded cheddar cheese, divided
- 1½ cups grated Parmesan cheese
- 2 cups panko bread crumbs

1. Preheat the oven to 375°F and lightly grease a 9 x 11-inch casserole dish.
2. In a medium sauté pan or skillet, heat the oil over medium heat.
3. Add the onion and sauté until translucent, 3 to 5 minutes. Add the Chick'n Wings and cook until lightly browned. Add the tomatoes and stir to incorporate.
4. Pour the tomato mixture into the prepared casserole dish and set aside.

5. Bring a large stock pot of water to a boil. Cook the pasta according to the package directions while you start to make the cheese sauce. If the pasta is done before the sauce, simply drain and set aside.

6. To make the cheese sauce, melt the butter in a large pot over medium heat. Whisk in the flour and cook until lightly browned and fragrant, about 2 minutes, whisking constantly.

7. Starting with ½ cup of the milk, whisk the milk into the flour mixture, incorporating it until smooth.

8. Add the mustard, basil, oregano, garlic powder, and salt. Reduce the heat to low and cook until it begins to slightly bubble, being careful not to boil.

9. Remove from the heat and whisk in 3 cups of the cheddar and the Parmesan cheese.

10. Add the cooked pasta to the cheese sauce and mix to combine. Spread the noodle mixture over top of the tomatoes.

11. Sprinkle the remaining 1 cup of the cheddar cheese and the bread crumbs over the top.

12. Bake for 25 to 30 minutes, until the cheese is bubbling on the edges and the bread crumbs are lightly browned.

Tater Tot Hotdish

What can I say–I'm a Midwestern girl and this is how we do it in Minnesota. The Tater Tot Hotdish could be emblazoned on the state flag. So it would be unacceptable for the vegetarians amongst us to be left out!

Makes 4 to 5 servings

- 2 tablespoons olive oil
- 1 small white onion, diced
- ½ recipe Ground Not-Beef (page 26)
- 2 cloves garlic, minced
- 8 ounces cremini mushrooms, chopped
- 2 tablespoons unbleached all-purpose flour
- 1 cup low-sodium vegetable broth
- ½ cup milk of choice
- salt and freshly ground pepper to taste
- 1 cup frozen peas, thawed
- 1 (2-pound) bag frozen tater tots

1. Preheat the oven to 375°F and lightly grease a 9 x 11-inch pan.
2. In a large sauté pan, heat the oil over medium heat. Add the onion and cook until translucent, about 5 minutes.
3. Add the Ground Not-Beef and cook until browned, about 5 minutes.
4. Add the garlic and sauté until fragrant, about 2 minutes. Transfer the mixture to a large bowl.
5. Add mushrooms to the sauté pan and cook until they release their juices.
6. Sprinkle flour over the mushrooms and stir to coat. Whisk in the vegetable broth and bring to a boil. Once it reaches a boil, lower to a simmer, add the milk, and

cook until it thickens, about 3 to 5 minutes. Adjust the seasoning to taste with salt and pepper.

7. Spread the not-beef mixture into the prepared casserole dish. Pour the mushroom mixture over it. Sprinkle with the peas and cover with a layer of solid tater tots.

8. Bake for 45 to 50 minutes, until the edges are bubbling and the tots are golden.

9. Let cool for 10 minutes before serving.

Spaghetti Squash Carbonara

Spaghetti squash is underappreciated, I think largely because people don't know what to do with it. This recipe balances a normally heavy dish with lovely squash, making for a lighter meal. Serve with a salad and bread.

Makes 4 servings

1 large spaghetti squash (about 2 pounds)

1 tablespoon olive oil

4 slices Seitan Fakin' Bacon (page 42), cut into small chunks

3 cloves garlic, minced

¼ cup low-sodium vegetable broth

2 egg yolks plus 1 whole egg

1 cup grated Parmesan cheese

salt and freshly ground pepper to taste

1. Preheat the oven to 375°F. Line a rimmed baking sheet with parchment paper.
2. Halve the squash and scrape out the seeds. Place cut-side down on the prepared pan and roast for 35 to 45 minutes, until the squash is tender at its thickest point when poked with a fork.
3. Remove from the oven and let cool to the touch. Using the tongs of a fork, scrape out the flesh into a large bowl. It will be stringy like spaghetti!
4. In a large sauté pan over medium heat, heat the olive oil, and cook the Fakin' until crispy, about 3 to 4 minutes.
5. Add the garlic and sauté until fragrant, about a minute. Transfer the Fakin' mixture to a bowl.

6. Add the vegetable broth to the pan and lower the heat to a simmer.
7. In a small bowl, whisk the eggs together with the cheese. Add a crack of salt and pepper.
8. Slowly whisk the egg mixture into broth, whisking rapidly to incorporate, just long enough to heat the eggs through.
9. Add the spaghetti squash and toss to thoroughly combine, cooking until the squash is heated through. Add the Fakin' mixture and toss to combine.
10. Adjust the seasoning with salt and pepper to taste and serve immediately.

Chicken Pot Pie

This timeless dish will make everyone happy the minute they see the flaky crust. Serve with a green salad and some crusty bread to sop up all the yummy sauce.

Makes 4 to 5 servings

2 tablespoons olive oil

1 small white onion, diced

½ recipe Basic Chick'n (page 14), diced

2 cloves garlic, minced

2 teaspoons dried thyme

2 tablespoons dried basil

2 small carrots, scrubbed and cut into ¼-inch coins

1 red bell pepper, seeded and diced

1 medium Yukon Gold potato, peeled and cut into ½-inch dice

1 teaspoon salt

½ cup frozen peas, thawed

1 cup low-sodium vegetable broth

1 tablespoon unbleached all-purpose flour

1 sheet puff pastry, thawed but still chilled

1 tablespoon melted unsalted butter

1. Preheat the oven to 350°F and lightly grease an 8-inch square casserole dish or a deep 8-inch pie pan.
2. In a large sauté pan, heat the oil over medium heat. Add the onion and cook until translucent, about 5 minutes.
3. Add the Chick'n and cook until browned, about 5 to 8 minutes.
4. Add the garlic and sauté until fragrant, about 2 minutes. Add the thyme and basil, and stir to coat the onions.
5. Mix in the carrots, bell pepper, and potato. Sprinkle with the salt.

6. Reduce the heat to medium-low and cook, covered, stirring often, until the potatoes and carrots are slightly softened, 10 to 15 minutes. You might need to add a splash of water occasionally to deglaze the pan. Add the peas.

7. In a small bowl, whisk together the vegetable broth and flour. Pour over the veggie mix and increase the heat to medium. Bring the sauce to a boil, then reduce the heat to low and simmer until the sauce starts to thicken, about 5 minutes.

8. Pour the veggie and Chick'n mixture into the prepared casserole dish. Cover the dish with the puff pastry, pressing it down firmly around the edges and trimming any excess as needed. Cut a vent in the middle of the pot pie and then brush the top with the melted butter.

9. Bake until the pastry is puffed and golden, 40 to 45 minutes. Let the pot pie cool for 15 minutes to set up before slicing and serving.

Galumpki (Cabbage Rolls)

As a child, I visited my great grandmother several times a month and it was not uncommon for her to greet me with a warm plate of galumpki. This meal is a Polish standby, one that every grandma has under her belt.

Makes 4 to 6 servings

- 1 medium head green cabbage
- ½ recipe Ground Not-Beef (page 26)
- 2 teaspoons olive oil
- 1 medium white onion, diced
- 3 cloves garlic, minced
- 2 cups cooked rice (about ¾ uncooked)
- 1 large egg
- 3 cups tomato soup, divided
- salt and freshly ground pepper to taste

1. Cut the core from the head of cabbage and rinse the leaves thoroughly.
2. Fill a stock pot with about 2 inches of water and bring to a boil over medium heat.
3. Add a sprinkle of salt to the water and place the cabbage, core-side down, in the water and cover. Cook until the outer leaves begin to look wilted, about 10 minutes.
4. Gently remove the cabbage from the water and rinse under cool water to stop cooking. Carefully separate the leaves and set aside on a plate lined with paper towels. Reserve the larger leaves, enough for the number of rolls you want to make, plus a couple of extras (about 15 to 18 leaves).
5. In a large bowl, combine the Not-Beef, olive oil, onion, garlic, rice, egg, and salt and pepper. Stir to combine.

6. Lightly spray a 9 x 11-inch baking dish with oil and pour half of the tomato soup on the bottom. Set aside. Preheat oven to 350°F.

7. Scoop ¼ cup of the Not-Beef mixture onto the bottom inside of a cabbage leaf. Fold the leaf's ends over the filling and roll up to tuck in the filling. Place seam-side down on the bottom of the prepared pan.

8. Repeat with remaining filling and cabbage leaves, tightly packing the cabbage rolls into a single layer. Coat the top with the remaining tomato soup.

9. Cover the pan with foil and bake for 45 minutes. Remove the foil and bake for 5 more minutes, until edges are lightly brown and the sauce is thick and bubbly.

Vegan variation: Replace the egg with ¼ cup of pureed tofu.

Assorted Sides

Whether you're looking for the perfect side dish or an accompaniment to round out your meal, you're in the right place.

Maple Fakin' Brussels Sprouts

Brussels sprouts have gone from childhood trauma to vegetable du jour overnight—and it's recipes like this that will keep you coming back for more. It's smoky, sweet, and with the cabbage-tang of the sprouts, you might want to make a double batch.

Makes 4 servings

1 pound brussels sprouts, rough ends trimmed and halved

3 tablespoons olive oil, divided

3 tablespoons maple syrup

2 cloves garlic, crushed

sprinkle of salt and freshly ground pepper

4 slices Seitan Fakin' Bacon (page 42), chopped

1. Preheat the oven to 400°F. Line a baking sheet with parchment paper and set aside.
2. Spread the brussels sprouts on the prepared pan and drizzle with 2 tablespoons of olive oil and maple syrup. Stir to coat, and add the crushed garlic and a sprinkle of salt and pepper.
3. Roast the brussels sprouts, stirring often, until tender when pierced with a fork, 25 to 30 minutes.
4. When the brussels sprouts are almost done, heat remaining olive oil in a large saucepan over medium heat.
5. Add the chopped Fakin' and stir to coat, cooking for 3 to 5 minutes, until the edges are golden.
6. Remove from the heat.
7. Transfer cooked brussels sprouts to a serving bowl. Top with Fakin' and serve.

Ultimate Mashed Potatoes

Mashed potatoes don't seem like they should be that hard, but we've all had incredibly bland, disappointing mashers. Don't waste any future mashed potato opportunities on underwhelming spuds. You can also use this recipe to make loaded mashed potatoes by adding 4 slices of Seitan Fakin' Bacon (page 42), shredded cheddar cheese, and a generous sprinkling of chives.

Makes 4 to 6 servings

- 2 pounds yellow or red potatoes, skins mostly peeled, cut into 1-inch cubes
- 3 tablespoons unsalted butter
- 2 tablespoons cream cheese
- 3 to 4 tablespoons milk of choice, as needed
- 2 cloves garlic, crushed
- salt and freshly ground pepper to taste

1. In a medium pot, cover the potatoes with water by about 1 inch. Bring to a simmer over medium-high heat and cook until the potatoes are tender when pierced with a fork, 15 to 20 minutes.
2. Drain the potatoes and place back in the pot, off the heat.
3. Add the butter, cream cheese, 3 tablespoons of the milk, and the garlic.
4. Mash the potatoes with a potato masher, incorporating the other ingredients until creamy.
5. Add more milk if needed. Season to taste with salt and pepper.

Miso Mushroom Gravy

This gravy is amazing poured over Chick'n Fried Steak (page 150), or on its own, pooled in the center of a mashed potato mountain.

Makes 2 cups

- 1 teaspoon mild vegetable oil
- 1 cup minced cremini mushrooms
- 2 tablespoons unsalted butter
- ¼ cup unbleached all-purpose flour
- 2 cups low-sodium vegetable broth
- 1 tablespoon mild (light-colored) miso paste
- salt and freshly ground pepper to taste

1. In a medium saucepan, heat the vegetable oil over medium heat. Add the mushrooms and cook, stirring often, until they release their juices.
2. Remove the mushroom pieces, but retain the liquid in the pan.
3. Add the butter and melt completely. Whisk in the flour. It will be thick.
4. Lower the heat to medium-low and stir often, until it smells slightly nutty, about 2 minutes.
5. Starting with just ¼ cup, whisk in the vegetable broth, working out any chunks. Add the remaining broth and increase the heat.
6. Stirring often, bring the mixture to a boil. Once boiling, add the miso and salt and pepper, and whisk to dissolve.
7. Lower the heat and cook until the mixture is slightly thickened, about 3 to 5 minutes. The gravy will thicken slightly more as it cools.
8. Add the mushrooms and stir to combine.

Pickled Vegetables

Pickled veggies are the quickest way to perk up a sandwich, salad, or cheese plate. They come together quickly and are a great addition to your fridge. Serve with Bahn Mi (page 112) or as part of an appetizer spread.

Makes 1 pint

1 cup water

1 cup unseasoned rice vinegar

¾ cup evaporated cane sugar

2 teaspoons salt

1 medium daikon, peeled and thinly julienned

4 large carrots, peeled and thinly julienned

1 large cucumber, peeled, seeded, and thinly julienned

1. In a medium bowl, whisk together the water, rice vinegar, sugar, and salt until the sugar dissolves completely.
2. Pack the daikon, carrots, and cucumber into a 1-pint mason jar, standing upright.
3. Pour the liquid over the veggies, moving them around a little to release any air bubbles and to make room for more liquid.
4. Refrigerate for at least 3 hours before using, but preferably a day or two. Veggies will keep in the fridge for up to 2 weeks.

Ultimate Cornbread

This recipe makes a lightly sweetened cornbread with a nice crusty exterior and a moist, fragrant interior, studded with pieces of actual corn throughout. Crumble over Ultimate Veggie Chili (page 80)—you'll feel pretty boss.

Makes 9 to 12 pieces

- 1 cup yellow cornmeal
- 1 cup unbleached all-purpose flour
- 2 tablespoons evaporated cane sugar
- 1 tablespoon baking powder
- ¼ teaspoon salt
- 1 cup milk of choice
- ¼ cup mild vegetable oil
- ¼ cup unsweetened applesauce
- ½ cup corn, fresh or frozen and thawed

1. Preheat the oven to 425°F. Lightly grease an 8-inch square pan with oil or line with parchment paper.
2. In a large bowl, combine the cornmeal, flour, sugar, baking powder, and salt.
3. In a small bowl, whisk together the milk, oil, and applesauce.
4. Add the wet ingredients to the dry and mix until just combined. Gently fold in the corn.
5. Spread the batter into the prepared pan and bake for 20 to 25 minutes, until golden and a toothpick inserted in the center comes out clean.
6. Let cool on a rack for at least 10 minutes before serving.

Buttery Biscuits

These biscuits will change your life. Seriously. Flaky, mile-high, and tender, they are the perfect sauce-sopping tool—especially with the Mighty, Meaty Minestrone (page 96)—and are equally suited to being slathered with more (!) butter and jam, if you're into it.

Makes 10 to 12 biscuits

- 2 cups unbleached all-purpose flour
- 1 tablespoon plus 1 teaspoon baking powder
- 1 tablespoon evaporated cane sugar
- 1/4 teaspoon salt
- 1 stick (1/2 cup) cold unsalted butter, cut into 1-inch chunks
- 3/4 cup milk of choice

1. Line a baking sheet with parchment paper and set aside.
2. In a large bowl, combine the flour, baking powder, sugar, and salt. Whisk to combine and remove any clumps.
3. Using a pastry blender or fork, cut the butter into the dry ingredients until a meal comes together. Add the milk and mix until just combined. The dough will look craggy, and that's okay.
4. Roll out onto a floured counter and knead a couple of times to work everything together. Fold the dough in half and roll out slightly. Fold again and roll out, and repeat 5 times total. This is how we'll get our flaky layers.
5. Roll out the dough to 1/2-inch thickness and cut out rounds with a biscuit cutter or the rim of a drinking glass, about 4 inches in diameter. Place on a prepared baking sheet, 1 inch apart. Collect scraps and use to knead together and form additional biscuits.

6. Preheat the oven to 450°F.
7. Refrigerate the biscuits for 15 minutes before popping in the oven. Chilling is essential to getting them to rise—the chilled butter will be shocked into evaporation when put in the oven, causing the dough to rise splendidly.
8. Bake for 11 to 13 minutes, until tall and golden. Let cool for a minute or two before serving.

Vegan variation: Replace the butter and milk with non-dairy alternatives.

Soda Drop Biscuits

These biscuits are a great tool to have in your box. They can be easily adapted to take on different flavors—add shredded cheese, garlic, or chives—or keep them simple for soaking up sauces. A delicious way to sop up Smoky Split Pea Soup (page 84).

Makes 6 to 8 biscuits, depending on size

1¾ cups unbleached all-purpose flour

½ cup quick-cooking or old-fashioned oats

2 teaspoons baking powder

½ teaspoon baking soda

¼ teaspoon salt

½ cup cold unsalted butter

½ teaspoon white or apple cider vinegar

1 cup milk of choice

1. Preheat the oven to 450°F. Line a baking sheet with parchment paper.
2. In a large bowl, combine the flour, oats, baking powder, baking soda, and salt.
3. Cut in the cold butter until it is incorporated and the flour resembles a coarse meal.
4. In a small bowl or cup, add the vinegar to the milk and let it sit for a minute to turn.
5. Add the milk to the dry ingredients and mix until just combined.
6. Drop onto the prepared baking sheet in large biscuits, about ⅓ cup of batter each, 1 inch apart.
7. Bake for 10 to 12 minutes or until the edges turn golden brown.

Vegan variation: Use non-dairy milk and margarine.

Happy Piggy Succotash

Nothing showcases the bright flavors of summer quite like succotash, particularly sweet corn, which plays delightfully off of the smoky fakin' bacon.

Makes 4 to 6 servings

- 3 teaspoons mild vegetable oil, divided
- 4 slices of Seitan Fakin' Bacon (page 42)
- 1 red bell pepper, diced small
- 2 cups lima beans, thawed if frozen
- 4 ears fresh sweet corn, cut off the cob
- 1 tablespoon olive oil
- 1 tablespoon apple cider vinegar
- 1 teaspoon evaporated cane sugar
- salt and freshly ground pepper to taste

1. In a large skillet, heat 2 teaspoons of the vegetable oil over medium heat. Cook the Fakin' until crisp, about 4 minutes, then set aside, cool, and cut into little bits.
2. Add the remaining vegetable oil to the pan. Add the bell pepper and lima beans, and cook until heated through but the bell pepper is still vibrant in color, about 5 minutes, stirring often. Add the corn and cook for another 2 minutes, stirring often. Transfer to a large bowl.
3. In a small bowl, whisk together the olive oil, vinegar, and sugar until the sugar is dissolved. Toss over the veggies and add salt and pepper to taste. Top with the Fakin'.

Fragrant Rice

This is an easy way to dress up your average rice, and it's not as labor-intensive as a biryani. It's a nice middle ground to add flavor and dimension without a lot of work. Serve with Seitan Masala (page 158) for a delicious meal.

Makes 4 to 5 servings

- 1 tablespoon mild vegetable oil
- 1 teaspoon ground turmeric
- ½ teaspoon ground coriander
- ½ teaspoon ground cinnamon
- ¼ teaspoon salt
- 2 cups uncooked basmati rice, rinsed
- 3 cups water
- ¼ cup golden raisins
- ¼ cup cashew pieces
- ¼ cup fresh cilantro, roughly chopped

1. In a large pot, heat the oil over medium heat.
2. Add the turmeric, coriander, cinnamon, and salt. Cook until fragrant, about 1 minute.
3. Add the rice and coat with the spice mixture. Lower the heat to medium-low and stir often, gently toasting the rice, about 5 minutes.
4. Add the water and gently stir to combine. Bring to a boil then cover and lower to a simmer.
5. Cook until the water is absorbed, without stirring, about 15 to 20 minutes.
6. Add the raisins on top of the rice, without stirring, and remove from the heat. Let the rice sit to fluff up for about 5 minutes.

7. Add the cashew pieces and gently fluff the rice with a fork, incorporating the raisins and cashews.

8. Mix in the cilantro right before serving.

Apple Sausage Stuffing

Serve this with Seitan-Tucken (page 138) for an incredible holiday meal, adorned with your other familiar sides.

Makes 6 to 8 servings

- 1 loaf sourdough or French bread, cubed or roughly torn (about 10 cups)
- ¾ cup dried cranberries
- 1 large sweet apple, such as Gala or Haralson, peeled, cored, and chopped
- 2 tablespoons olive oil, divided
- ½ recipe Italian Sausages (page 34), cut into coins and then into half moons
- 1 large yellow onion, finely diced
- 3 tablespoons finely chopped fresh sage
- 1 tablespoon finely chopped fresh rosemary
- 1 teaspoon chopped fresh thyme
- ½ cup pecans, chopped
- ½ cup fresh parsley, chopped
- 1 cup white wine
- 3 tablespoons unsalted butter
- 2 cups low-sodium vegetable stock
- 1 egg, lightly beaten

1. Preheat oven to 350°F. Divide the cubed bread between two baking sheets. Bake 10 to 15 minutes, stirring the bread occasionally, until toasted but not browned.
2. Place the toasted bread cubes into a very large bowl, then add the cranberries and apples. Set aside.
3. Grease a 9 x 13-inch casserole dish with butter or mild vegetable oil. Set aside.
4. In large skillet over medium heat, heat 1 tablespoon of the olive oil and cook the sausage until lightly browned,

about 3 to 5 minutes, stirring often. Remove from the pan and add to the bowl with bread.

5. Add the remaining olive oil to pan. Add the onion and cook, stirring often, until translucent, but not browned, about 5 minutes, stirring often. Add the sage, rosemary, and thyme, and stir to combine. Remove from the heat and add to the bread mixture. Add the pecans and parsley.
6. Add the wine to the skillet and scrape the browned bits from the bottom of the pan as it cooks. Add the butter and vegetable stock. Bring to a boil, then remove from the heat and pour over the bread cubes in bowl. Add the egg. Toss gently until combined, and spread into the prepared baking dish.
7. Cover the pan with tin foil and bake for 40 minutes. Remove the foil and bake 15 minutes more, until the top is browned.

Vegan variation: Omit the egg. Use non-dairy margarine. Increase the broth by an additional 2 tablespoons.

Garlic Bread Twists

These are amazing with soup, but also make a great side for a heartier salad—try them alongside Steak Salad (page 111) or sop up the sauce from your Galumpki (page 174). Chock-full of garlic, these twists are delicious (maybe not a first date recipe, though).

Makes 6 to 8 breadsticks

- ½ (2.25-ounce) package rise yeast (1⅛ teaspoons)
- ¼ teaspoon sugar
- ½ cup plus 1 tablespoon warm water
- 1½ cups unbleached all-purpose flour
- ½ teaspoon garlic powder
- 2 teaspoons olive oil
- 3 tablespoons butter, melted, divided
- 6 to 10 cloves garlic, minced (as desired)
- sea salt, for sprinkling

1. In a large bowl, combine the yeast, sugar, and ¼ cup of the warm water. Let sit for a few minutes until frothy.
2. In another bowl, combine the flour and garlic powder.
3. Add the rest of the water and oil to the yeast mixture and begin to incorporate the flour ½ cup at a time. Mix until a sticky dough forms.
4. Roll out onto a floured surface and knead until a smooth, elastic dough forms, adding flour as needed. The dough should be moist, but not sticky.
5. Place dough in an oiled bowl, turning once to coat. Cover and let rise until doubled in size, approximately 45 minutes.

6. Preheat the oven to 400°F and line a baking sheet with parchment paper.
7. Punch the dough to deflate, and turn out onto a floured surface.
8. Divide dough into 3 equal parts. Divide each of those into 2 equal parts. Roll each piece of dough into a long rope, about 10 to 12 inches long. With a rolling pin, flatten each rope.
9. Prep two small bowls, one with 2 tablespoons of melted butter and the other with the minced garlic. Brush each flattened rope with melted butter and sprinkle evenly with minced garlic. Fold over one side of rope to touch the other and seal.
10. Bring ends together, pinching the ends and bring sides of dough next to each other, making a flattened O shape. Twist the breadstick twice and transfer to the prepared baking sheet.
11. Repeat with the remaining dough, placing the breadsticks 2 inches apart on the baking sheet.
12. Bake for 12 to 15 minutes or until lightly browned.
13. Remove from the oven and let cool for a minute or two before brushing on the remaining melted butter.
14. Sprinkle with sea salt and serve warm.

Vegan variation: Replace the butter with non-dairy margarine.

Ham and Potato Wedges

Serve as a side dish, or the wedges are impressive on their own. Warm or cold, for breakfast, brunch, lunch, or dinner—you can't really go wrong. You'll need a cast-iron pan to get the crusty edges, and this recipe alone is worth the investment if you don't have one already.

Makes 6 to 8 servings

- 4 pounds Yukon gold potatoes
- 4 tablespoons melted unsalted butter, divided
- 1 small yellow onion, cut into very thin half moons
- 3 tablespoons fresh thyme, chopped
- ½ recipe Basic Ham (page 18), sliced thin
- 3 tablespoons balsamic vinegar
- salt and freshly ground pepper to taste

1. Preheat the oven to 450°F.
2. Peel the potatoes then slice into ⅛-inch slices.
3. Heat 2 tablespoons of the melted butter in a 10-inch cast-iron skillet over medium heat. Add the onion and cook until translucent, about 5 minutes. Remove from the heat.
4. Spread the onions evenly across the bottom of the skillet. Arrange one layer of potatoes in a concentric circle on top, then sprinkle with salt, pepper, and 1 tablespoon of the thyme.
5. Add half of the ham slices to make a solid layer on top of the potatoes.
6. Drizzle with 1 tablespoon of the vinegar.

7. Repeat with the potatoes, salt, pepper, and thyme, then the remaining ham. Drizzle the remaining melted butter over the ham, then 1 more tablespoon of the vinegar.
8. Add one last layer of potatoes. Drizzle with last tablespoon of vinegar, then more salt, pepper, and the remaining thyme.
9. Cover with tin foil, then transfer the skillet to the oven for 30 minutes.
10. Carefully remove the skillet from the oven and remove tin foil. Press down on the top of the dish firmly with a spatula.
11. Return the pan to the stove over medium-low heat. Be careful, as the pan will be very hot. Continue cooking, occasionally pressing down with the spatula, until a fork easily pierces the potatoes in the center, about 15 to 20 more minutes.
12. Remove from the heat and let cool slightly.
13. Run a small knife around the edge of the skillet to loosen, then flip out onto a cutting board to cut into wedges. Transfer to a serving platter.

Roasted Cabbage Wedges

A great side for a heavier meal, this incorporates veggies in a unique way to mix things up. Leaving the core in makes the cabbage easier to cook, and your guests can cut away the core when eating.

Makes 4 to 6

1 small green cabbage (about 1 pound)

1 tablespoon olive oil

3 tablespoons unsalted butter

1 small shallot, minced

2 cloves garlic, minced

2 tablespoons Dijon mustard

1 teaspoon honey or agave

salt and freshly ground pepper to taste

1. Preheat the oven to 450°F. Line a baking sheet with parchment paper.
2. Cut off the rough end of cabbage. Remove any exterior leaves that are damaged.
3. Cut the cabbage in quarters from top to bottom. Then cut each quarter half to make 8 wedges.
4. Place the cabbage wedges on the baking sheet and drizzle with olive oil. Add a little salt and pepper.
5. Roast for 5 to 8 minutes, then flip the wedges and roast on the other side, until lightly browned and core is tender when pierced, about 5 to 10 more minutes.
6. Meanwhile, in a small saucepan, melt the butter over medium-low heat. Add the shallot and cook until fragrant, about 2 to 3 minutes, stirring often. Add the garlic and cook for 1 to 2 minutes longer. Remove from the heat and whisk in the mustard, honey or agave, and

a little salt and pepper. Add a little water if the sauce is too thick.

7. To serve, place the wedges on a platter and drizzle with the sauce. Serve immediately.

Vegan variation: Replace the butter with non-dairy margarine.

Conversions

Volume Conversions

U.S.	Metric
1 tablespoon / ½ fluid ounce	15 milliliters
¼ cup / 2 fluid ounces	60 milliliters
⅓ cup / 3 fluid ounces	90 milliliters
½ cup / 4 fluid ounces	120 milliliters
1 cup / 8 fluid ounces	240 milliliters

Weight Conversions

U.S.	Metric
1 ounce	30 grams
⅓ pound	150 grams
1 pound	450 grams

Temperature Conversions

Fahrenheit (°F)	Celsius (°C)
140°F	60°C
150°F	65°C
160°F	70°C
350°F	175°C
375°F	190°C
400°F	200°C
425°F	220°C
450°F	230°C

Recipe Index

Acknowledgments

Thanks to Jesse, for always being game to try new things and for being constructive with your feedback. To the amazing readers of my old blog, for your continued support and enthusiasm. To the fine folks at Ulysses Press, for giving the opportunity to play with purpose in my kitchen for all these years. And to my grandmothers, even many years after you've left this earth, you continue to teach me so much, in and out of the kitchen.

About the Author

Kris Holechek Peters is the author of many vegan cookbooks, including *The 100 Best Vegan Baking Recipes, Have Your Cake and Vegan Too, The I Love Trader Joe's® Vegetarian Cookbook, Vegan Desserts in Jars,* and *Vegan Ice Cream Sandwiches.* Kris learned how to cook and bake at the feet of her grandmothers and continues to refine her skills under the watchful eyes of her feline overlords.